hillary kerr & katherine power

WHAT to WEAR, Where

the how-to handbook for any style situation

WHAT to WEAR, Where

FOREWORD BY NICOLE RICHIE

the HOW-TO HANDBOOK FOR ANY STYLE SITUATION

BY HILLARY KERR & KATHERINE POWER

ABRAMS IMAGE | NEW YORK

TABLE *Of* CONTENTS

FASHION *fundamentals* *10*

date: first *46*

*f*OREWORD

by nicole richie

When it comes to fashion, there are very few rules that apply to everyone, all of the time. However, I think we can all agree that it's important to know what to wear for any occasion. As a girl, when you hear about an event, the first thought that goes through your mind is: "What should I wear?" As silly as it may sound, wearing the right outfit will give you a certain feeling of power and security. Plus, it's always an opportunity to express different aspects of your personality. When you think about it that way, you won't get anxious, and you just might enjoy the process—which is exactly how it should be.

Aside from that, creating the perfect look is one of the best parts of the occasion itself. Take the opera, for example: the preparation—putting on a gown, picking the right accessories, creating your beauty look—is what makes this event exciting and gets you in the right mood. Would the opera still be the opera without the dress and the jewelry and the glamour? In my opinion, it would be incomplete, and what's the point of going somewhere if you're not going to get the full experience?

For these reasons, *What to Wear, Where* is an absolute must-read. It's an invaluable resource for anyone who has wondered if she has dressed appropriately for a specific occasion or even if she just wants to add something extra to her everyday style. As the cofounders of the online fashion magazine WhoWhatWear.com, Hillary and Katherine are super skilled at breaking down the latest fashion trends and explaining how to make them your own, rather than simply knocking off the latest look. They've brought that expertise to this helpful book, which is full of their down-to-earth, practical, and accessible style advice.

With that in mind, I am pleased to introduce *What to Wear, Where*.

Nicole

DEAR READERS,

Y ou know it's happened to you: the invitation to your high school reunion arrives in the mail, the person you've been swooning over finally asks you out, or your resume catches someone's eye and you get the interview. You open the envelope, answer the phone, reply to the email, and say, "Yes! I would be delighted to attend/I'm free on Saturday/I'd love to come in for an interview." Then it hits you: what in the name of all that's holy—Christian Louboutin, Chanel, and Kate Moss—are you going to wear?!

First things first: don't freak out.

Yeah, right. Okay, freak out a little bit, but don't go into full-blown panic mode, because you're holding all of the answers. That's right, *What to Wear, Where* has all the solutions for your most stressful style situations—it's like an emergency hotline for any wardrobe worry! Whether it's an everyday occurrence (dog park!) or an uncommon outing (opera!), *What to Wear, Where* is full of tips and tricks for creating the perfect look for any event and will help you tackle all of the trickiest social occasions.

And how do we know all of this information? Well, as the cofounders of the celebrity and runway style website WhoWhatWear.com (and as fashion magazine editors prior to that), we've dedicated our careers to compiling style secrets and gathering fashion insights from famous tastemakers, star stylists, and top designers. We've also spent years studying all of the best celebrity and runway looks, deciphering the key elements that make these outfits work, and translating these hard-won truths into our own real-girl wardrobes.

Now, before we delve into the heart of *What to Wear, Where*, a quick note about what you'll find inside. In each chapter, we discuss all the things you need to consider when creating a look for a particular occasion, and we show you what we'd wear in that situation. Please bear in mind that our outfits are only suggestions and that there are certainly thousands of other equally appropriate options. In fact, your ensemble doesn't need to resemble ours in the slightest—do your own thing! In other words: Don't get hung up on the colors, silhouettes, or even the overall vibe of any of our looks. Instead, just focus on the ideas behind these combinations and let those big-picture guidelines inform your own clothing choices. The results will be great (we promise) and hopefully you'll enjoy the process, too. After all, life is stressful—your outfit shouldn't be!

Hillary & Katherine

fASHION fUNDAMENTALS

Before you start putting together an outfit, it's always a good idea to think about your wardrobe goals for this particular occasion. Sometimes it helps to have a cheat sheet, so we've compiled this short checklist of basic ideas to get you started. It's simple, sure, but sometimes that's all the inspiration you need to create an amazing look!

1 LOCATION: *Where you are going? What will the climate, venue, lighting, and overall environment be like?*

2 ATTENDEES: *Who will be there?*
Let the guest list guide you! *Are your fellow guests conservative lawyers or hipster artists? Families with small kids or single adults?* **If you have friends who are going too, don't forget to talk to them about what they're wearing.**

3 FABRICS: *Are they appropriate?*
Did you pick a heavy wool suit for a July job interview? Are you thinking about wearing a satin evening dress to a daytime event?

④ TAILORING: *Do your clothes fit correctly?*
Do your hems drag on the ground?
Is your jacket too snug?
If the fit isn't right, it's the wrong thing to wear.

⑤ BALANCE: *Is your skin-to-clothing ratio correct?*
Are you showing lots of skin from the waist up?
If so, are your legs covered?

⑥ PRESENTATION: *Do you look neat?*
Is your shirt wrinkled? Are your shoes scuffed or missing
heel tips? **These small details are so important!**

⑦ BEAUTY: *Are you appropriately groomed?*
Are you wearing makeup suited to a Girls' Night Out
on a Casual Date? Do you have chipped, dry nails?

⑧ CURRENT TRENDS: *Does your outfit*
include one of-the-moment piece?
Even if you're wearing timeless essentials,
an au courant piece of jewelry or on-trend jacket
can completely change your look.

Dinner Party ·······

······· Engagement Party

······ Country Club

Courtroom

Country Club

Music Festival

Opera

EVERY OCCASION A to Z

ART GALLERY

Oscar Wilde once wrote that you "should either be a work of art, or wear a work of art," a sentiment that's worth remembering when getting dressed for an Art Gallery event. Now that doesn't mean you should turn up in paint-splattered canvas per se, but you should feel free to break out a few of your bolder pieces. That's the great thing about this social situation—aside from the ubiquitous bottles of white wine or soul-lifting inspiration one hopes to find, of course—you're definitely allowed, even encouraged, to experiment with your ensemble. *Your goal is to create an outfit that shows your personality in a creative and sophisticated way.*

Regardless of your personal style, your footwear is of paramount importance when attending a party or show at an art gallery because you're going to be on your feet for this whole event. Platform booties are perfect for this very reason: you get the ideal combo of heel height, comfort, and style! Again, since your fellow attendees typically fall under the category of "creative types," this is a great time to break out your more directional accessories, whether that's statement jewelry, an of-the-moment bag, or fashion-forward shoes.

We both opted for vibrant outfits for our Art Gallery looks, but don't let the bright colors throw you. Hillary started with a really simple foundation: a slightly oversized silk blouse, skinny jeans, and the aforementioned ankle boots. To personalize the ensemble and make it more interesting, she added loads of bohemian accents, including a wide-brimmed hat, peacock-feather–print scarf, and numerous necklaces. These add-ons bring a touch of psychedelic style to her wardrobe essentials, and the results are totally art-show appropriate.

Katherine's ensemble has a very different vibe, but it's just as easy to execute. Since Art Gallery events are usually in the early evening, she decided to take one of her work outfits and simply funk it up a bit. She untucked her lady-like blouse and knotted it at the waist, and then she swapped her office-appropriate heels for some of-the-moment lace-up booties. Again, the fundamental pieces are quite straightforward—a blazer, blouse, and a miniskirt—but Katherine used a combination of prints, textures, and styles to make her outfit interesting.

BEAUTY BOX

Typically art galleries are very well lit. While that's great for seeing the art, it can also make you look overdone in the makeup department. Don't turn up with a full face of heavy makeup; instead keep things light and fresh with natural lipstick or lip gloss, dewy skin, and unfussy hair.

" *You're definitely allowed, even encouraged, to EXPERIMENT with your ensemble.* "

OTHER OUTFIT IDEAS

1 blazer + leather skirt or shorts + silky t-shirt + ankle boots

2 miniskirt or dress + opaque black tights + lightweight print scarf

3 slim black pants + kimono top + long interesting necklaces

GO FOR

bold colors; mix-and-match patterns; texture; workwear separates paired with edgier pieces; slim jeans or pants in gray or black; print or vibrant skirts; feminine blouses; platform ankle boots or wedges; oversized clutches; slouchy hobos; print scarves; statement jewelry

STEER CLEAR

super-casual clothes; sweats; voluminous skirts or dresses; suits (mix your work basics with something dressier or edgier); uncomfortable shoes; heavy makeup

RISKY BUSINESS

sequins (can work in small doses, like a glitzy bolero thrown over a burnout t-shirt); low-cut necklines; blue denim (black or gray is dressier); cocktail dresses (temper it with something casual, like a vintage denim jacket); flats

BARBECUE

YOUR goal is to create a look that's casually cute and subtly on-trend with at least one FLIRTY element.

There are a lot of social events that offer the wardrobe equivalent of memorizing verb tenses in Latin or cleaning out your refrigerator—a bore or a chore—but getting ready for a summer barbecue is always a delight. Whether it's on a friend's rooftop or in your own backyard, these warm-weather afternoon events always offer the trifecta of fun: sun, sizzling food, and the opportunity to show some style. Plus, you get to break out the carefully curated collection of little dresses, killer sandals, and summery shirts you've been buying all spring. Your goal is to create a look that's casually cute and subtly on-trend with at least one flirty element. Unlike for Picnic or Beach/Pool events, you can wear your light or white dry-clean–only frocks (just watch out for BBQ sauce and grass stains), as well as other higher maintenance items like strappy sandals, wedges, and your favorite handbags. Two more must-haves every barbecue look should include: sunglasses and some sort of lightweight outerwear option.

While you certainly can wear your favorite summer sundress, we wanted to show you two looks that centered around another warm-weather necessity: shorts. Katherine went for a vintage-inspired look via a cuffed pair of high-waisted khaki shorts and a cropped cotton bustier. The shorts have a relaxed silhouette and a hint of menswear tailoring, which make them the perfect counterpoint to an ultrafeminine top with lingerie details. This duo is a great, slightly dressier alternative to her other favorite barbecue look: a flowy tank dress and a bandeau bikini. Finally, since it's important to bring along a lightweight outerwear option, Katherine grabbed her go-to shrunken denim jacket for when the sun goes down.

To create an even more casual barbecue-appropriate ensemble, Hillary decided to start with a wardrobe essential: jean shorts. Since the jorts are a little tomboyish, she added some femininity via a body-skimming crocheted top and denim wedges. Hillary finished her outfit with another utilitarian piece, her favorite worn-in surplus jacket, simple aviators, and a soft leather bucket bag.

BEAUTY BOX

Hot weather and heavy makeup do not go together, so be sure to lighten up your beauty routine! SKIN: Use tinted moisturizer with SPF coverage and translucent powder on your t-zone, followed by blotting papers later in the day. EYES: Go for water-resistant or waterproof mascara. If eyeliner is a must, pick up a smudge-free, long-wear formula. LIPS: Skip the lipstick and use lip tints or stains instead.

OTHER OUTFIT IDEAS

1. delicate tank + colorful bikini top + cutoffs + woven sandals

2. crochet dress + denim jacket + raffia wedges

3. strapless maxi dress + bright or embellished flip-flops + statement earrings

4. high-waisted denim shorts + tucked-in tank + straw fedora + strappy sandals

GO FOR

slouchy, soft tanks and t-shirts; brightly colored bikinis; strapless maxi dresses; denim or khaki shorts; linen drawstring pants; kimonos or bed jackets; semi-sheer cardigans; denim or army jackets; wedges; clogs; strappy sandals; woven moccasins; big totes or long-strap bags; lightweight scarves; chic sunglasses

STEER CLEAR

anything with a lot of studs or hardware; flannel; body-conscious dresses; multi-strap tops or dresses (bad tan lines); tons of jewelry; heavy makeup (it will smear—not cute)

RISKY BUSINESS

wearing black (go for a thin fabric, like cotton or chiffon, and balance it with denim or light neutrals); silk (shows sweat easily); miniskirts (go for a full skirt, not a body-con version)

ACCESSORY ESSENTIAL

SUNGLASSES!
An on-trend pair of sunglasses will instantly update your basics and make you look fashionable. Invest in a new, of-the-moment style every summer.

BEACH & POOL

Looking chic at the beach or a pool can be about as easy as finding a new bathing suit—in other words, not very. You want to look casual and effortless, without erring on the sloppy side, yet your outfit can't be too sophisticated, lest it gives off that dreaded trying-too-hard vibe. Rather than making a major mistake, most girls just go for their tried-and-true getups, and cover up with either a print pareu or a worn-in pair of cutoffs and the first flip-flops they can find. There's nothing wrong with these options—they're totally fine—but we wanted to give you some alternatives that are a little more sartorially advanced. *The goal is to create a look that can seamlessly transition from the surf to the turf in a stylish, skin-covering way.* Our formula is simple: no matter if you're hitting the sand or simply lounging poolside, a great swim look always involves the following four items: a cute sun hat, an oversized beach bag, cool sunglasses, and the right suit.

When prepping for the beach, keep in mind that this environment is tough on your swimwear, so don't break out your most fashionable, expensive, and delicate options. It's also important to make sure your suit is appropriate for saltwater activities and will stay in place when you're frolicking in the waves. As far as your cover-up goes, lightweight layers in machine-washable fabrics are always a great choice. Katherine picked a gauzy long-sleeve button-up and a relaxed pair of draped shorts, which she can wear in a number of different combinations. The accessories really pull her look together: a straw fedora (adds flair), tan huaraches (a great alternative to flip-flops), and a fun multi-fabric tote (holds all the essentials). Oversized sunglasses are the perfect finishing touch.

Assembling a poolside outfit is a bit easier since you have fewer practical concerns to deal with and can wear something with a little more flair. You can wear a suit that offers more form than function, but make sure you pick a smart cover-up (something easy to pull on, but also appropriate and chic enough to wear to a café for lunch). Hillary likes a tunic or caftan in silk or super-sheer cotton for these situations. While it's certainly acceptable to opt for a solid color cover-up, a bold print is always a savvier choice, so feel free to experiment with patterns: tie-dye, ikat, tropical, watercolor—you name it! Again, make sure you have a stylish sun hat: it's a piece that's really worth investing in. Look for something in a lightweight, flexible material (you want a hat that bounces back if it gets squashed), ideally with a wide brim.

BEAUTY BOX

The beach/pool is the perfect time to experiment with braids, buns, and new-to-you updos. Use the natural texture you get from the ocean to create beachy waves, or after a dip in the pool, slick some conditioner in your hair and twist it into a chignon. Just try something!

"A great swim look ALWAYS involves the following items: a cute SUN HAT, cool sunglasses, and the RIGHT SUIT."

OTHER OUTFIT IDEAS

1. men's chambray shirt with cuffed sleeves + straw fedora + black slip-on sandals

2. string bikini + cotton tank + long sarong worn as a skirt + flip-flops

3. denim cutoffs + thin cotton batwing top + flat espadrilles

GO FOR

thin, oversized button-ups worn over your suit (for extra cuteness: cuff your sleeves twice, then scrunch them up over your elbows, and pop your collar); denim cutoffs; sheer maxi dresses; full skirts; flat sandals; totes or across-body bags in vibrant fabrics or natural materials; straw/canvas sun hats

STEER CLEAR

anything that has to be dry-cleaned; heavy fabrics; body-conscious skirts or dresses; stilettos; closed-toe shoes; strappy sandals that buckle or lace up; leather bags with heavy hardware

RISKY BUSINESS

black (go for sheer, soft fabrics with feminine details); metallics (just a hint or you'll look over the top); linen (wrinkles); t-shirts (you don't want a farmer's tan); fine jewelry

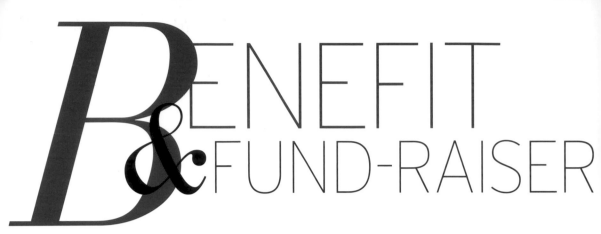

BENEFIT & FUND-RAISER

Whether it's for political purposes or simply to raise awareness for a personal cause, at some point you will be called on to attend some sort of benefit or fund-raiser. Obviously the cause is of paramount importance, so you don't want to detract from the purpose of said event by showing up in something totally inappropriate. To honor the situation, you must dress with some sense of gravitas—this is not a Girls' Night Out nor is it a Fashion Event—but you still should be able to infuse your outfit with a little personality, too. Proper doesn't mean bland, boring, or blah! *The goal is to create a sophisticated outfit that would also work for most business events.*

For a daytime event, Hillary wanted to put together a look that would be appropriate for both the philanthropic world and the office. Rather than reaching for bright colors or bold patterns, she stuck to a classic palette of gray, cream, and black. Sober hues are best for these events—anything fluorescent, vivid, or pastel can be tricky. Silhouette-wise, it's better to err on the traditional side, hence her selection of a knee-length dress and tailored jacket. Obviously a dress isn't your only option; a slim pencil skirt and a blouse would be appropriate, too, or you could go for a pair of high-waisted,

WARDROBE ESSENTIAL

INVESTMENT DRESS

It's always important to have one go-to dress in your closet that can work for a wide range of occasions. Ideally, it should be able to seamlessly transition from day to night, so look for something with a timeless cut and seasonless fabric. Additionally, the dress should have a modest neckline and a knee-length hem (slightly above or below is fine).

wide-leg trousers. If you're worried about not being formal enough, a good guideline to follow is to make sure there's at least one structured item in your outfit. Another way to show that you understand the seriousness of the occasion is via your accessories: a structured bag and a ladylike pair of heels convey something different than a slouchy hobo and flip-flops, right?

If it's a nighttime event, you have a little more freedom to put the fun in fund-raiser, as Katherine's outfit suggests. Of course, properness is still key, so make sure that the base of your look is timeless. A classic sheath, shift, or column dress is always acceptable for these occasions; just make sure it's in a fancier fabric, meaning no cotton, jersey, or denim. If you want to wear a shorter hemline à la Katherine, remember to cover your arms and décolletage. As for your accessories, this is definitely where you get to show your taste and reveal your style. An oversized sequin clutch is a wonderful way to work a little sparkle into your outfit. Or you can take a page from Katherine's playbook and add color, texture, or pattern via your footwear. She opted for a timeless shape—peep-toe pumps—in an unexpected hue, which is the perfect balance of propriety and pizzazz.

OTHER OUTFIT
IDEAS

1 pencil skirt + silky blouse + peep-toe pumps + structured bag

2 fitted sheath dress + sharp-shouldered blazer + closed-toe heels + quilted chain-strap purse

3 tailored pantsuit + feminine shell + vintage cocktail ring + oversized clutch

GO FOR

neutral colors (gray, black, navy, brown); long-sleeve or cap-sleeve dresses; fitted pantsuits; feminine shells and blouses; pencil skirts; structured jackets; tailored dresses; ladylike bags; peep-toe pumps; one piece of statement jewelry; vintage jewelry

STEER CLEAR

denim; wild or vibrant prints and patterns; strapless dresses; miniskirts; floor-length dresses (unless it's a black-tie benefit); biker jackets; strappy platforms; boots; edgy accessories

RISKY BUSINESS

bright colors; prints and patterns (unless it's a spring/summer luncheon); sequins or metallics (only use in small doses unless the event is black-tie); suits (you'll need to dress up your suit with a festive top and noncorporate accessories)

Birthday PARTY

FACT: No matter how big or small the celebration may be, every girl wants to look AMAZING on her birthday.

Though it may sound silly, what you wear on your birthday might be one of the most important annual outfits you create—no wonder it leads to so much stress and tears! But remember, no one wants you to cry in your cake, so try to enjoy the process a little, okay? ***The goal is to create a festive, fabulous outfit with a little bit of drama.*** Remember, this is your night, so create a look that combines some of your favorite essentials with a new knockout piece.

Your birthday suit, if you will, should be a bit dressier and feel more special than what you'd wear for a Girls' Night Out, but still have some of that trendy, outrageous spirit.

Also keep in mind that the key is to feel über-confident, so pick whatever sort of silhouette or style works for you: cocktail dresses, sexy skinny pants, major miniskirts, or glam jumpsuits! It's also important to bring a little sparkle into your look one way or another. That can mean a rhinestone cocktail ring for some, a shimmery top for others, or even a full-on sequin dress.

> **"** *It's important to bring a little sparkle into your look one way or another.* **"**

OTHER OUTFIT IDEAS

1 silky jumpsuit + statement waist belt + strappy sandals

2 sequin miniskirt + super-thin t-shirt + cropped leather jacket

3 short, full skirt + silky print tank + peep-toe ankle boots

4 lace dress + statement lipstick + metallic sandals

5 black leather pants + sequin tank + cage sandals

GIRLS' NIGHT OUT—PG. 68

SIDE NOTE: *As a guest, you should look festive, but remember: don't overshadow the birthday girl! It's still important to spend some time on your outfit—it's a sign of respect!—but now is not the time to wear your most embellished, sexiest, or boldest outfit.*

"Create a *LOOK* that combines some of your *FAVORITE ESSENTIALS* with a new *KNOCKOUT* piece."

Whatever you wear, just make sure that it's a look that truly shows off your personality. For example, Katherine prefers an understated femininity to anything ultra-girly, so she picked a short flouncy dress, then balanced the sweetness of said frock by keeping the color palette appropriately sober. She threw on her favorite black leather jacket—a wardrobe essential— and added some sparkle via glittery pumps and a couple of chunky rhinestone bracelets for party-perfect results!

Now Hillary, on the other hand, has never met a sequin or a spotlight she didn't like, so she embraced glamour wholeheartedly. Though her dress has a ton of sequins, they're metallic, so the party frock looks sophisticated and chic. Another good tip when you're wearing so much sparkle: balance the boldness with neutrals. For example, temper a dramatic dress with subtle heels instead of flashy shoes. Hillary picked a pair in a color that's in sync with her skin tone; they look harmonious with her dress and lengthen her legs—two great things!

GO FOR

bright colors; ruffles; embellishments; fancy fabrics; leather; directional shapes; dramatic draping or volume; sheer accents; cocktail dresses; short, swingy skater skirts; silky jumpsuits; faux-fur outerwear; clutches; bold costume or rhinestone jewelry; embellished headbands

STEER CLEAR

daytime fabrics like cotton or jersey; corporate clothes (have some fun!); jeans; your go-to LBD; basic t-shirts; flats; daytime bags

RISKY BUSINESS

big/bold prints (there will be lots of pictures from that night, so if you want to wear that outfit again, people will be less likely to remember a solid); blazers (choose one with sharp shoulders or interesting embellishments and wear over a fancy frock)

BEAUTY BOX

Much like on a Girls' Night Out, you can totally go for a bolder beauty look on your birthday, but make sure you do a test run for your prospective hair and makeup. You'll probably take a zillion pictures that night, so you want to make sure you look fabulous on camera. Plus, since it is a big night, you don't want any bad surprises.

BOWLING
(& other activities...)

THE goal is to create an outfit that lets you indulge in the nostalgic fun, while still looking MODERN.

There comes a time in everyone's life when the amusements beckon and certain activities turn up on the agenda: bowling, miniature golf, arcade games—you get the picture. Whether you find yourself in some sort of Lebowski-quoting hipster bowling league, going for a round of putt-putt at a kid's birthday party, or playing Whac-A-Mole on the boardwalk, you still need to assemble an ensemble that's cute and speaks to your personal style. The goal is to create an outfit that lets you indulge in the nostalgic fun, while still looking modern. The look should be somewhat on par with something you'd wear for Errands, but with a few practical ramifications. Also, we encourage you to embrace your chosen game by wearing items that reference that activity.

Obviously this topic is somewhat broad, and what's critical clothing-wise when playing skee ball may differ slightly from the wardrobe essentials one needs to rack up strikes and spares. That said, there are some general outfit guidelines that are worth noting and following. Pants are key; go with a movement-friendly pair, meaning jeans with some stretch or slightly loose chinos (boyfriend-cut styles are great). Of course you could choose casual shorts, too; just follow the same guidelines we mention for denim! Also, you might

have to swap out your shoes for regulation gear, so pick cropped or easily cuffed bottoms and make sure you're either wearing socks or you have a pair in your bag. Machine-washable fabrics are also appropriate for these types of events; that way, if you accidentally spill your Slurpee or get sweaty playing Dance Dance Revolution, it's no big deal.

For Katherine's activity outfit, she wanted to make sure she had an equal balance of fashion and function, so she grabbed her favorite easy-fit jeans, cuffed the hems (this instantly makes low-top tennis shoes look cute), and put on one of her wardrobe essentials—a plaid button-up shirt. As a nod to her personal taste, she added a long-strap bag in a bright violet hue for contrast and a touch of femininity. It's also a smart choice because the exaggerated strap means she can wear it as a cross-body purse and keep her hands free for the activity.

While Hillary may be better at quoting The Dude than knocking down pins, her outfit is also appropriate for these game-oriented outings. As a high-heel devotee, she refused to go for sneakers, instead opting for a walking-friendly wedge. Though her leather jacket might not seem like an obvious choice, this jacket allows for movement and only looks better with age, so it can stand up to whatever the occasion holds.

OTHER OUTFIT
IDEAS

1 cuffed dark blue jeans + white tee + soft leather loafers

2 denim Bermuda shorts + cuffed plaid button-up + oxfords

3 knee-length retro dress + flats + cropped leather jacket

GO FOR

machine-washable fabrics; relaxed silhouettes; lightweight layers; cuffed jeans or khakis; thin button-ups; denim vests or jackets; soft, slouchy outerwear; socks; sneakers; cross-body bags

STEER CLEAR

Irreplaceable items; miniskirts; hot pants or short shorts; white pants; low-rise pants; bell-bottoms or flares; low-cut tops; blazers; stilettos; long necklaces; chunky bracelets or rings; heirloom jewelry

RISKY BUSINESS

maxi skirts; dresses (a casual, cotton, mid-length sundress could work for putt-putt); shorts (be wary of culottes or cutoffs); skinny jeans (make sure they're stretchy, not too low-rise, and that you're wearing them with a longer top); sandals, wedges, and flat boots (make sure you bring socks)

CORPORATE COCKTAIL PARTY

The corporate cocktail party can be a bit high pressure, as it's a treacherous situation to navigate—socially and sartorially—with lots of room for error. Plus, the stakes are high: it's bad enough to look inappropriate at a normal party, an embarrassing but forgettable offense, but making a poor clothing choice in front of your superiors and colleagues can have long-lasting ramifications. We're not overstating it: if you show questionable judgment in the wardrobe department, your boss will wonder if you're making mistakes in other areas, too. *The goal is to transform a business-appropriate outfit into a work event ensemble by changing your accessories.*

When getting dressed for a corporate cocktail party, remember that this is not an off-duty event, so don't think that you can let loose. Just because martinis may be on the menu doesn't mean you're going to order four of them and then start freaking Mark from legal, does it? No! Stick to classic pieces you'd wear to the office—blazers, modest dresses, pencil skirts, interesting blouses—spiffed up with slightly more extravagant accessories. For Katherine, that means starting with a simple base outfit: a long-sleeve little black dress made up of lots of sheer layers. The semitransparent fabric is opaque enough to be appropriate for a work-related function and is a nice choice for nighttime. To ramp up the professionalism of the outfit, she added a conservative suit blazer. Katherine accessorized with a rhinestone necklace and a patent clutch to give the look some glamour and show her personal taste, before finishing the ensemble with a pair of glittery black heels. (Black is key; the same silhouette in silver or red would be a huge mistake.) Remember: you can really have the most fun with jewelry, so feel free to try a standout piece.

If your field errs on the more conservative side, you might prefer to play with texture instead of adding glitz via your accessories. Use Hillary's outfit as your reference point: she picked a formfitting black pencil skirt as the foundation of her corporate cocktail outfit, and then she added a white blouse with lace details. It's a more feminine and interesting alternative to the classic button-up, plus the dramatic high collar and full sleeves add some personality to this traditional piece. Since the blouse is a bit of a statement on its own, she added sheen via a patent leather belt and bag. That texture implies dressiness in a very subtle way. One final note: go for a minimal beauty look—polished hair and classic makeup—just like you would for a job interview.

> **SIDE NOTE:** *Transforming a more risqué outfit into something that's appropriate for work is easy. To make your outfit office-ready, add a jacket; a strapless dress, slightly-too-bare silk tank, or body-con sheath can look professional when worn under a structured blazer. Black opaque tights are another go-to trick if your hemline feels a mite short; they also ground gauzy t-shirts or dresses.*

OTHER OUTFIT IDEAS

1   black/gray slacks + simple shell + embellished bolero

2   dark shift dress + statement belt + opaque tights

3   pencil skirt + slim patent leather belt + ruffled/feminine blouse + crisp blazer

GO FOR

dark colors; traditional silhouettes with a twist; blazers; tailored dresses; pencil skirts; interesting blouses; classic pumps; clutches; patent leather belts, bags, and shoes; accessories with a touch of shimmer or shine; a single statement piece of jewelry; opaque or sheer tights

STEER CLEAR

informal fabrics (knits, jersey); showing too much skin; the exact same thing you wore to work; the exact same thing you would wear to a club; miniskirts; club shoes; daytime shoes; daytime bags; jewelry overload; trendy makeup

RISKY BUSINESS

bright colors; sequins (use sparingly); sheer pieces (make sure you're covered); trendy shoes; costume jewelry (limit it to one strong conversation piece)

FESTIVE!

COCKTAIL PARTY

Break out your martini shakers, dear readers, because it's time to discuss that time-honored tradition: the cocktail party. Now, we know that there are about as many different reasons for having a party as there are cocktail recipes—zillions—but the cause for celebration isn't really important. What does matter is that you know how to create an outfit that looks as good as a perfectly cold cocktail tastes: in a word, marvelous! So whether the fete is to ring in the holiday, toast someone's accomplishment, or simply meet new people, you need to look lovely. *The goal is to create a saucy outfit that suits you perfectly and alludes to the night's festive mood in a subtle way.*

In our opinion, nothing says "Why yes, I'd love a drink" like a little sparkle, which is why festive cocktail ensembles should always involve our favorite fancy neutrals: metallics. While pale metallics, like champagne and light silver, can work, they can also look cheap, so if you're not 100% confident in your choice, always go for darker iterations—gunmetal, pewter, and copper—instead. Of course, you also don't want to look like a disco ball gone mad, so pick a single metallic piece and then use dark neutrals to tone it down. The perfect festive outfit calls for a combination of different textures, so be sure to use a range of fabrics/materials. For example, you could wear an embellished jacket (sparkle) with a silk shirt (luster) and skinny black pants (matte).

For Hillary, festive cocktail attire requires a spirited frock, so she found a metallic brocade dress for this occasion. Since the dress has an ultra-girly, vintage vibe—especially with the gift-bow belt!—she added a black leather bolero. This piece toughens up the outfit's overall look and infuses the ensemble with some modernity. Hillary finished her look with an embellished clutch and peep-toe pumps; these items also add a mix of matte and sparkle to her outfit, achieving the cocktail-party combo perfectly!

Katherine's outfit is also fantastic for a celebratory fete, and it happens to follow our festive formula, too! The focal piece of her look is an oversized sequin tee, which she styled with a pair of matte black skinny jeans to create a very modern mix. To ensure she doesn't feel underdressed—most women will be in skirts or frocks—she added luster everywhere via pointy glitter pumps and a long rhinestone-encrusted pendant. She also swapped her black day bag for its after-hours counterpart, the clutch, to complete her cocktail-party look.

> **SIDE NOTE:** *Whenever you have a cocktail party—or any social situation, really—consider the four Ws: who, what, when, and where. Ask yourself WHO will be going/hosting? WHAT are we celebrating? WHEN is this event, time-wise? WHERE is the event? Regardless of the occasion, answering these questions will give you a little direction when creating your outfit.*

OTHER OUTFIT IDEAS

1 black party dress + vibrant print pumps + cropped metallic coat

2 silver mini dress + red lips + black patent pumps + camel coat

3 tulle dress + cropped faux fur coat + velvet pumps

GO FOR

metallics, sequins, and embellishments; cocktail dresses that embrace the current trends; little leather jackets; sparkly tops, blazers, or skirts; slim black pants; eye-catching bags; party clutches; ultra-sexy pumps; peep-toe ankle boots; embellished stilettos; rhinestone statement jewelry

STEER CLEAR

informal fabrics; dull outfits; daytime outfits; kitschy holiday-themed pieces; blue denim; suits; corporate clothes; day bags

RISKY BUSINESS

floor-length dresses (a maxi can work but make sure it's not too dressy); flats (we highly suggest heels, but we know some people never wear them; if you must go flat, make sure the shoes are appropriate for nighttime, meaning sparkly or patent leather)

Cold WEATHER

Have you ever noticed that there's something about blustery weather that brings out people's boring side? Just walk down any New York street—or anywhere it's freezing—come fall's first frigid winds and all you'll see is a sea of black jackets, black parkas, and black puffers. It's dull to look at and it's dull to wear. In times like these, it's all about covering up in a cute way. *The goal is to create an outfit that uses a mix of multicolored layers and texture for a surprising and stylish look.*

Not all layers are created equal: you need to think about the right combination of textures, fabrics, tones, and fit in order to avoid looking like the Stay Puft Marshmallow Man.

In addition to using color and texture to create a visually pleasing ensemble, remember that cooler climes allow you to go nuts with the accessories! We highly suggest that you experiment with hats, gloves, and belts to enhance your outfit, especially if you're a little fashion-phobic; these small but powerful pieces give you a lot of bang for your buck, sarto-

OTHER OUTFIT IDEAS

1) flannel button-down + leather pants + soft scarf + coat

2) black opaque tights + metallic skirt + black sweater + charcoal coat

3) skinny jeans + over-the-knee boots + silky top + chunky snood + wool coat

rially speaking. Also always think about how you can reinterpret your wardrobe essentials for cold weather. Oftentimes you can get more wear out of your lightweight pieces by simply combining them with other thin layers. For example, you can wear a beloved pair of open-toe leather wedges as you transition into fall simply by styling them with a pair of socks! (Note: this only works with darker neutral colors and seasonless materials like leather; don't try this with, say, white peep-toe espadrille wedges.)

For Hillary's cool-weather ensemble, she started with a combination of two outfit essentials: medium-blue jeans and a light chambray shirt. With that blue-on-blue foundation settled, she threw on a chunky cable-knit sweater and an oatmeal jacket with abbreviated sleeves. To ensure she stayed warm and to punctuate her outfit, she added a chocolate brown hat and cozy black gloves. The mixture of complementary tones is super-stylish, plus she gets to prolong the life of her wardrobe staples, a good deal all around.

ACCESSORY ESSENTIAL

PLATFORM BOOTIES!

Though it might seem counterintuitive, a platform boot or bootie is one of your best bets for a cold-weather ensemble. (Please know we don't mean they're the right pick for a heavy blizzard situation, but they are good when the weather is frigid but snow-free.) The platform acts as insulation for your foot—boosting it up and away from the freezing sidewalk—and keeps the chill at bay.

> *Experiment with hats, gloves, and belts to enhance your outfit; these SMALL but POWERFUL pieces give you a lot of bang for your buck.*

SLOUCHY KNIT BERET!
Chapeaux are cold-weather necessities, but they're also responsible for that dreaded look: hat head. If you want to avoid this condition—and really, who doesn't?—make sure you have a loose-fit cashmere beret in your accessory arsenal. It's the secret to keeping your head warm without ruining your hair.

"Texture IS KEY when you're working with layers and neutral colors; IT'S THE easiest way to add interest to an otherwise bulky ENSEMBLE."

Katherine decided to put together a look that is very unbasic black to showcase a dressier option. Her ensemble can easily go from day to night, which is key if you're running around all day or going from work to play. That said, she started with a pair of wool shorts over thick wool-blend tights, which allows her to show her shape and embrace a trend, while staying warm. Next she selected a charcoal gray, body-conscious turtleneck sweater; in addition to being a wonderful wardrobe staple, it's also a great layering piece. You can wear it alone, with other sweaters, or under spring dresses when the weather starts to warm up slightly. Over this stylish foundation, she added a lightweight black wool coat and cinched it at the waist with an interesting elastic belt to give her silhouette some shape. The lightweight coat is an essential: it's a transitional piece that works from fall through the beginning of winter, and then again at the end of winter. It's also slim enough to layer under something bulkier when it's truly freezing. (The elastic belt is another excellent cold-weather accessory, because it adjusts itself no matter how many layers you're wearing.)

Then it was time for the last outerwear layer: a textured gray wool coat. Texture is key when you're working with layers and neutral colors; it's the easiest way to add interest to an otherwise puffy and bulky ensemble. With her outfit sorted, it was time to move on to accessories! In addition to picking a cold-banishing pair of ankle boots, Katherine accented her outfit with a loose cashmere beret, leather gloves in a rich berry hue, and a brown long-strap bag.

GO FOR

neutral colors; deep jewel-tone accents; body-conscious sweaters for layering; long wool cardigans; belted lightweight coats; thick wool overcoats with interesting silhouettes (strong-shouldered, oversized, bell, military) and textures (chunky knit, nubby wool, faux fur); puffer coats with belts; dark denim; boots with thick soles or platforms; bags with longer shoulder or across-body straps; thick opaque wool tights; long thick scarves in a cool print; thick elastic or other adjustable waist belts that will fit over your many layers; cashmere berets; beanies; felt fedoras; leather or cashmere gloves

STEER CLEAR

all-black basics; light colors; summer fabrics; sheer tights

RISKY BUSINESS

distressed denim (the holes in your jeans will let in cold air; if you love the look, wear your opaque tights underneath); open-toe wedges (styled with a pair of socks, these shoes are a viable option for blustery fall days)

CONCERT

The goal is to create a movement-friendly outfit with lightweight layers and at least one ON-TREND element.

First, a disclaimer: this chapter is about what to wear to a concert, singular. If you're looking for outfit ideas for what to wear to a multi-day, multi-band show—you know, the kind that takes place in a field—check out our Music Festival recommendations instead. That said, whether you're catching an intimate set in a tiny club (Hillary) or going to a mega-show to dance your face off (Katherine), remember that this is an excellent occasion to experiment with your look. A concert usually means you're going to be with friends, in an anything-goes environment, so use this opportunity to take a style risk.

Of course, there are some practical consider-

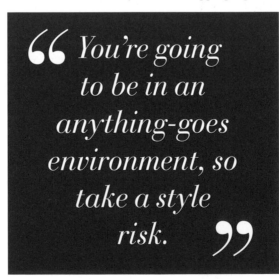

" You're going to be in an anything-goes environment, so take a style risk. "

ations to keep in mind, too: it's always a good idea to wear something that allows for dancing, which means skipping super-constricting pieces. Secondly, the temperature can vary at a venue, so pick a versatile outfit that works whether you're hot or cold. The goal is to create a movement-friendly outfit with lightweight layers, and at least one on-trend element.

Nine times out of ten, when Hillary goes to a show, it's at some small club, which means she can dress up a bit more. Jeans are the foundation of the look, but instead of basic blue denim—which is definitely expected in this situation—she grabbed a black skinny pair with some stretch. Then she

BEAUTY BOX

There are so many social situations when your hair and makeup must be appropriate, but a concert is not one of them! Have fun and feel free to experiment with an extreme hairstyle you've wanted to try or a dramatic beauty look. Regarding the latter, just be sure you pick water-resistant formulas for your eye makeup (a little smudging is okay, lots is just trashy), go easy on the foundation (base + sweat = gross), and wear whatever you want on your mouth.

OTHER OUTFIT IDEAS

1 leather pants + striped top + denim jacket + sparkly pumps

2 black dress shorts + graphic tee + sparkly draped jacket + ankle booties

3 sparkly tank + faux fur vest + black skinny jeans + pumps

4 high-waisted bell-bottoms/flare jeans + tucked-in t-shirt + cropped suede jacket

5 romper + across-body bag + fringed ankle boots

added a flowy tank in an of-the-moment print, a tissue-thin oversized button-up as another lightweight layer, and topped everything off with a cropped leather moto jacket.

To give her outfit a little texture, she picked a long-strap fringe bag, which can be worn over the shoulder or across the body, and black glittery heels. Heels might not seem like a practical choice—and they're not, really—but if you find a comfortable pair that you don't mind standing in all night, why not?

For Katherine, a concert means lots of dancing, so she started her outfit with a super-comfortable graphic-print tunic and a draped, dark gray vest. Since the tunic is quite short, she added a pair of leather shorts for some extra coverage to ensure she can throw her hands in the air and wave them like she just don't care—er, if you will.

> *"It's always a GOOD idea to wear something that allows for DANCING, so skip super-constricting pieces"*

Next, Katherine toughened things up with her accessories, starting with a pair of platform ankle boots. Keep in mind that you want to make sure your shoes are not only chic, but also foot-friendly, too, since you never know if you'll have to walk a mile for parking or if you'll end up dancing nonstop for three hours. She gave her outfit a little more rock attitude with a studded belt, chain necklaces, and finished the whole thing off with a black leather satchel. Again, it has a long strap, so she can wear it across her body and not have to worry about where it is all night. It's also big enough for some supplies, like a lightweight jacket or scarf for after the sun goes down.

ACCESSORY
E S S E N T I A L

ACROSS-BODY BAG

Sometimes worrying about your handbag is a real hassle. In situations like this, the across-body bag can be a lifesaver. Any-time you're going to an event that calls for lots of activity or movement—a concert, music festival, bowling—make sure you grab a long-strap bag.

GO FOR

studs or grommets; prints (stripes, plaids, polka dots, dark bohemian florals); skinny jeans with stretch; distressed jeans; flowy tanks; lightweight button-ups; tunics; leather jackets; leather shorts or pants; draped vests; platform ankle boots; comfortable heels; motorcycle boots; across-body bags; scarves; tough accents like chain necklaces

STEER CLEAR

blazers; work attire; cocktail dresses; flip-flops (no one likes crushed toes); large or long coats; uncomfortable shoes; clutches or handheld bags

RISKY BUSINESS

miniskirts (if you plan to stand on your seat or have to climb lots of steep stairs, minis can be a major problem); hats (they can look cool, but can obstruct your fellow patrons' view, so keep them low profile)

MUSIC FESTIVAL—PG. 90

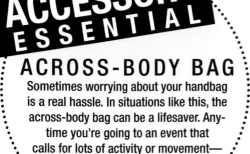

COUNTRY CLUB

Generally speaking, if you hear the word "club," you immediately associate it with one of only a few things: nightlife, golf, books—or sandwiches, if you're hungry. But while it might not immediately come to mind, the country club is certainly worth consideration, especially since it's one of the few places you'll ever go that has a literal, not simply suggested, dress code.

Whether it's in the Hamptons or Houston, Miami or Malibu, superchic or *Caddyshack*-esque, putting together a country club look isn't complicated, as long as you know the rules. The goal is to create a polished outfit that's a cut above your favorite casual look. Of course, some clubs are much more conservative than others, so before getting dressed, make sure you know exactly what is permitted and what is not allowed.

Most country club events take place during the day and often outside, so it's generally best to stick to lighter colors and fabrics (no all-black outfits). Flats and wedges are always appropriate, as are modest hemlines and necklines, minimal accessories, and easy beauty looks. Remember that many members are there for the tennis courts or golf course, so if you want to get into the athletic spirit and wear something white or with sporty details, feel free to do just that.

For her country club look, Katherine went with a striped long-sleeve t-shirt, her favorite mid-length trench, and a cute pair of patterned shorts. The shorts are a darling choice for a number of reasons: the wide-leg style is a flattering option for most women, the print is certainly livelier than a pair of solid Bermudas, and the hemline is modest (as far as shorts go) but modern. She kept the outfit's summery spirit going with her accessory choices, too. The tan wedges and brimmed straw hat are timeless essentials, while the interlocking belt and ladylike white bag add a touch of seventies chic to the whole look.

> 66 *The goal is to create a POLISHED outfit that's a cut above your favorite casual look.* 99

Modern classics were on the menu for Hillary as well. Instead of wearing khakis, she picked a full skirt in a similarly neutral hue for the foundation of her outfit. As for her tops, she started with a very classic, crisp white blouse (a sleeveless style, in this case) and then added an embellished cardigan in a sunny coral hue for a little oomph. Instead of heels, she selected an espadrille wedge and accessorized with a cork bag—the material makes the clutch a perfect daytime choice—and tortoiseshell sunglasses.

OTHER OUTFIT IDEAS

1. knee-length colorful dress + tan sandals + tan clutch
2. pastel shift dress + gold ballet flats + neutral cardigan
3. khaki/chino shorts + white button-down + dark belt + lace-up espadrilles
4. wrap dress + flat sandals + cardigan

GO FOR

stripes; preppy fabrics, like madras or seersucker; anything with sporty style; trench coats; cuffed Bermuda shorts; bright cardigans; flats, like loafers, moccasins, and ballet-inspired styles; wedges or espadrilles; ladylike day bags; oversized clutches; interesting belts; straw fedoras

STEER CLEAR

cleavage; body-con styles; jeans or jean shorts (while some clubs allow "premium denim," the lines are very blurry here so play it safe); short shorts; tracksuits; crop tops; evening bags; club shoes; oversized hats

RISKY BUSINESS

strapless tops or dresses (make sure you have a cardi or cropped trench standing by); tank or halter tops (some clubs don't allow them); denim jackets, vests, or dresses; high heels

COURTROOM

The GOAL is to create a polished and professional outfit that would WORK in a corporate business setting.

Unless you are a super-stylish, high-powered attorney, we hope you never have to go to court. That said, if you ever receive a judicial summons, it certainly behooves you to answer said call in a perfectly proper outfit. The key words to keep in mind are classic, modest, and serious; you need to show you understand the magnitude of the situation and are respectful of the legal system. The goal is to create a polished and professional outfit that would work in a corporate business setting. Remember: this is not a fashion show, it's a trial, so lock up your fashion-forward tendencies and make sober style choices instead.

Whether you're testifying, simply attending court proceedings, or getting slapped with a SCRAM bracelet, your outfit should always be conservative. If you want to wear a dress, like Hillary, it's always a good idea to pick something knee-length and with sleeves, ideally in a solemn color like navy, gray, or black. Additionally, make sure you pick a fabric that's appropriate for daytime. A black wool dress definitely says something different than the same frock in satin (too fancy) or jersey (too casual).

Closed-toe pumps are an appropriate choice, as is a structured bag; just be sure to keep the number of accessories to a minimum. A trim belt adds polish to a businesslike dress, but be wary of anything that makes too much of a statement. The same holds true for jewelry; you don't want to wear your gaudiest baubles; stick to understated items like small pearl or diamond studs, a simple gold or silver bracelet, or one classic ring. Hillary, for example, wanted to limit the amount of information her accent items communicate, so she simply opted for a very classic tank watch—a professional and timeless pick.

Of course pants are a completely appropriate option, too; just make sure you mimic Katherine and wear them in a ladylike and chic way with minimal accoutrement. (Think: power suit, but not pushy.) She picked a feminine buttoned-up blouse—nothing too sheer, tight, or low-cut—with an elegant pair of slacks and a classic blazer.

As she so deftly demonstrates, you don't have to wear an all-black outfit; neutrals are an equally dignified choice. Because she wants to communicate how put-together she is in all areas of her life, Katherine added an oversized clutch in a complementary color and a pair of neutral pumps. Dark sunglasses will provide a bit of protection as she goes from the car to the courtroom—an essential finishing touch, indeed!

OTHER OUTFIT
IDEAS

1 charcoal pencil skirt + forest-green silk blouse + black blazer + pointy pumps

2 black shift dress + black opaque tights + dark neutral cardigan + closed-toe heels

3 slim trousers + crisp button-down (tucked in) + slim belt + blazer

GO FOR

dark neutrals like gray, navy, and black; modest hemlines; a suit or suit elements; cardigans; pencil skirts; crisp button-ups; feminine blouses in solid colors or muted florals; long-sleeve dresses; closed-toe shoes with a modest heel; understated accessories; minimal makeup

STEER CLEAR

bright colors, especially red; anything sheer; bold patterns or prints; anything sleeveless; body-conscious silhouettes; sequins or other flashy embellishments; denim of any kind; miniskirts; maxi dresses; t-shirts; flats; sandals; severe heels (anything too high, strappy, or with too much hardware); excessive jewelry; hats

RISKY BUSINESS

open-toe shoes (a peep-toe is safe, but sandals should be skipped)

Date: CASUAL

Is there anything harder than coming up with the perfect casual-date outfit? We'd rather create 100 looks for the opera or 50 different corporate job interview options before we'd willingly attempt a low-key date ensemble. Whether you're going to a weekend movie or rendezvousing at the local coffee shop with your crush, the correct casual-date outfit isn't always an obvious choice—and there are endless wardrobe options. Talk about a nightmare! And, if that's not enough, you want to look chic, sexy, and adorable, but you can't overdo it because you know he'll be in jeans and a t-shirt. *The goal is to create an outfit that is together, yet effortless, and shows your figure in an understated way.* Don't forget this is a date, so you should include some slightly flirty elements in your look.

The key to any date is to be comfortable in what you're wearing, as this is essential to feeling confident and carefree. As such, a great jumping-off point for your outfit is to start with your favorite casual item—sweatpants excluded, of course. That means the beloved jeans that you wear every day and have perfectly formed to your body, your brother's old concert tee that you've worn to shreds, or a simple sundress that makes you feel fabulous. From there, we also suggest trying to incorporate at least one feminine element in your outfit, whether that's a girly floral print or a blouse with a hint of lace or a delicate necklace.

For Katherine's casual-date outfit, she picked one of her go-to summer dresses: a little floral number that hints at her figure. She added a cozy element to her outfit with a thick cardigan, which

WARDROBE ESSENTIAL

LITTLE LEATHER JACKET

Investing in a little leather jacket is one of the smartest things you can do. It's an incredibly versatile piece: use it to toughen up a girly outfit, add some cool to a cocktail party ensemble, or simply throw it on with your favorite jeans and a vintage t-shirt for the perfect off-duty look.

OTHER OUTFIT IDEAS

1 perfectly worn-in vintage t-shirt + short full skirt + nude flat sandals

2 skinny jeans + semi-sheer draped tank + slouchy vest + motorcycle boots

3 print shorts + snug tank or t-shirt (tucked in) + moccasins + jean jacket

GO FOR

muted florals/liberty prints; anything with subtle lace details; sheer or silky tops; your perfect jeans; wedges; moccasins; ballet flats; flat, strappy sandals; flat or wedge boots; delicate jewelry; soft makeup and touchable hair

STEER CLEAR

anything too trendy (save that for a Girls' Night Out); anything too tight or short; sequins or other embellishments; sweatpants or other baggy bottoms; high heels; hats

RISKY BUSINESS

animal print (it works in small doses, like a belt or scarf, any more than that feels too aggressive); loose tops or dresses (you want to show your shape, so if you must go flowy, add a belt to cinch the waist); blazers (choose a cropped or shrunken style and wear with something more feminine)

not only looks approachable, but also will keep her warm in an air-conditioned movie theater or on an evening stroll. As for footwear, she went for wedges—the ideal casual-date shoe. They're the perfect way to get a little height, easy to walk in, and they don't look as fancy as a pump. Plus they're cute in leather, cork, or jute and look darling styled with a pair of socks à la Katherine. Speaking of which, the socks are a playful addition to her outfit, and they show her style and personality, as does her cool vintage bag.

Hillary, on the other hand, opted for a very classic combo—jeans and a leather jacket—for her low-key date look. While the pairing is timeless, she kept things current by opting for jeans in a medium-blue hue (the lighter wash is inherently more casual than a dark-rinse style) and picking a slim, cropped jacket in dark copper leather. The jeans and the jacket are both pretty fitted, so to balance that out and add a dash of femininity to the outfit, Hillary added a gauzy cotton camisole with lace details. The top is girly without being overly sweet, and the peekaboo panels are subtly sexy. While flats would be fine with this outfit, Hillary likes shoes with height, so she went for a pair of raffia wedges instead. She finished her outfit with a few fun bracelets (some sentimental picks, others simply for style) and a gray chain-strap hobo bag.

Date: FIRST

The GOAL is to create a slightly dressy outfit that combines FLIRTY elements with touches of toughness.

Oh, the fun of a proper first date! It's not "hanging out," nor are you doing some sort of spontaneous activity; we're talking about a preplanned dinner date. How exciting, how nerve-wracking, and how on earth are you ever going to figure out what to wear? You are a grown-up—in theory, at least—so you know that this is the time to step it up from your jeans-and-a-sexy-top combo that worked so well in high school or college.

That said, you don't want to seem like you tried too hard and spent all day in the salon or look overdressed to the point of ridiculousness. The goal is to create a slightly dressy outfit that combines flirty elements with touches of toughness. The look should be relatively similar to what you'd wear to work in a creative office, but with more nighttime-appropriate touches and sex appeal.

And remember that this isn't the night to experiment with the latest crazy silhouette or over-the-top runway trend. It will be wasted on most men and can even alienate a few, so save those looks for the next Girls' Night Out.

While there are certainly lots of cute trousers or perfectly nice dresses you could pick, we think the most fail-safe option is to go with a skirt. Oftentimes, a dress is just a little too "done" for a date, while pants don't necessarily convey the right flirty attitude. Of course these aren't hard-

> *" Having a wardrobe crisis? Just pick your favorite body feature, highlight it, then balance the rest of your look from there. "*

BEAUTY BOX

As a rule of thumb, men dislike obvious makeup. Instead of breaking out a glossy red lip, err on the natural side, meaning: flirty lashes, glowing skin, a little blush, and a pinky-nude lipstick with a creamy texture and a slight sheen. Touchable hair is a good thing, too, so whether you like a blowout or soft curls, keep the product to a minimum.

OTHER OUTFIT IDEAS

1 cuffed tapered pants in a silky fabric + fitted tank + studded pumps

2 dress shorts + lace blouse + stilettos

3 tank dress + waist belt + lightweight cardigan + lace-up booties

4 tan bandage skirt + black racer back tank + black suede ankle boots + denim jacket

5 dark floral dress + leather moto jacket + nude pumps

6 black leather pants + thin white tank + denim jacket

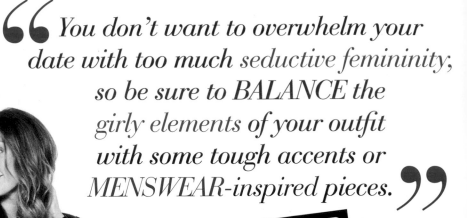

"You don't want to overwhelm your date with too much seductive femininity, so be sure to BALANCE the girly elements of your outfit with some tough accents or MENSWEAR-inspired pieces."

GO FOR

touchable materials; a mix of feminine and masculine pieces; prints balanced with solid colors (like black tights); belled skirts; ruffled minis; tucked-in tops, like simple shells, tanks, and t-shirts; heels (pumps, wedges, or ankle boots); a tough accessory or two; one conversation piece of jewelry; natural hair and makeup

STEER CLEAR

dowdy, baggy separates (you want to show off your body a little); über-trendy pieces; anything uncomfortable (how can you relax otherwise?); anything too tight or sheer; turtlenecks; suits or office attire; maxi dresses; sticky gloss or lots of heavy lipstick

RISKY BUSINESS

jeans (if you must, go for a dark wash); pants (stick to fitted silhouettes or balance with a flirty top); blazers (wear with a feminine skirt so you don't look like "work"); skintight minis (pair with a baggier tank or t-shirt)

and-fast rules; there are obviously a number of appropriate options. What matters most is that you feel comfortable and confident—as we mentioned in Casual Date.

One easy way to help determine your outfit is to pick your favorite body feature, highlight it, then balance the rest of your outfit from there. For example, if you love your legs, opt for a shorter hemline, but make sure your neckline is high and/or you cover your arms. If you adore your décolletage, then choose a lower-cut top, but make sure it's either loose or paired with a modest skirt.

We also recommend going with heels in this style situation. Unless you are one of those girls picked one of her favorite black party skirts (read: short and poofy), while Katherine opted for a short, slightly ruffled/tiered option in a black-and-white print. The neutral pattern keeps the skirt from heading into froufrou territory, as does the abbreviated hemline. Since Hillary's wearing black opaque tights, she wanted to show a hint of skin, so she opted for a silky print tank with a slightly scooped neckline. Katherine took the opposite approach: her legs are bare so she went for a more modest t-shirt and blazer combo. The blazer is a good pick, as it adds a little masculinity to her outfit.

Your accessories are another great place to add

> ## "This ISN'T the time to experiment with the LATEST crazy silhouette or over-the-top RUNWAY trend—save those looks for your next Girls' Night Out."

who swears she can't walk in anything other than flats, you should step it up (literally) and pick a shoe with a mid-to-high heel. Also, you don't want to overwhelm your date with too much seductive femininity, so be sure to balance the girly elements of your outfit with some tough accents or menswear-inspired pieces.

Finally, remember that you want to show your personality through your outfit, so pick your accessories carefully. Sure, your date might not be able to fully grasp that you're a preppy career girl because of your pearl earrings and simple gold bangles or that your double-finger studded ring is a nod to your tough tomboy side, but on some level he'll get it. (Or he won't, but you will!)

As for our favorite first-date outfits, as mentioned before, we both swear by skirts. Hillary some attitude to your look. Sometimes just one piece with studs, grommets, or heavy hardware can be all you need to give your outfit a touch of edge. For example, Hillary's silver-studded belt de-sweetens her outfit, while Katherine's buckle booties give hers another element of downtown cool. Finally, when considering your jewelry and beauty look, we implore you to keep things simple. Of course, you should be yourself—just not your most extreme self.

> **SIDE NOTE:** *While we suggest staying away from jeans, if you want to make your outfit a little more casual, add a denim piece. A chambray shirt, denim jacket, or denim pencil skirt can tone down a dressy look in seconds.*

OTHER OUTFIT
IDEAS

1. chiffon maxi dress + beaded sandals + bangles

2. black harem pants + silky tank top + peep-toe booties + denim jacket

3. dark skinny jeans + ladylike blouse + pumps + chain link bracelet

GO FOR

unusual colors or silhouettes; silky, slouchy pants or tanks; maxi skirts; leather jackets; shrunken blazers; cardigans; wedges; ankle booties; flowy dresses; cocktail rings; chunky necklaces or layered chains; oversized scarves

STEER CLEAR

delicate or light fabrics; denim (unless this is super-casual, see below for more details); leggings (opt for slim black pants instead); body-con dresses or skirts; crisp button-ups

RISKY BUSINESS

dressy fabrics or anything embellished; jeans (if you are going to a close friend's house for a very casual dinner on a Sunday night, go for dark denim, otherwise step it up a notch); flats (unless you are the hostess—but make them festive)

DINNER PARTY

While we always love a rager, go gaga for galas, and are bananas about casual barbecues, there's something so delightful about a simple dinner party. Whether it's an intimate at-home gathering or a festive group at a restaurant, the dinner party is one of those lovely in-between events—not so casual, but not fussy-fancy either—that never stress us out in a bad way. Sure, you want to look darling, but because it's a pretty laid-back affair, you don't need to worry about being perfectly appropriate. *The goal is to create an outfit that is fun, fashionable, and appropriate for the venue and hostess.* It should be a bit more fashion-forward than your First Date look, but not as trend oriented as a Girls' Night Out ensemble.

Unless your hostess is planning some sort of theme, typically the at-home dinner party is a bit more relaxed than the restaurant version. Also, because you're in someone's abode, know that you will probably be helping in some way and then flopping around on the furniture after eating, so you want to put a look together that embraces these active, comfortable surroundings. Accordingly, Katherine created an outfit that epitomizes the idea of effortless chic via a pair of silk pants in a gorgeous rust color and two layered tanks—one solid and one print—as the foundation of her outfit. The draped fit of these pieces matches the relaxed environment of her dinner party, but the combination of the fancier fabric and interesting colors makes it seem a bit dressier. Instead of picking a traditional heel, Katherine chose a great pair of lace-up ankle boots and tucked the top of her pants into the shoes, creating a harem effect. In keeping with the casually cool spirit of this occasion, she also added a soft, lightweight cardigan, some interesting jewelry, and a vintage-inspired navy blue suede clutch.

If the dinner party in question is being hosted at a restaurant, obviously it's important to find out how fancy the location is before sorting out your outfit. That said, it's nice to pick something a little festive, so now is a good time to break out a more dramatic or on-trend silhouette, play with a bold print, or add an edgy accessory. For her dinner party look, Hillary opted for a fabulous floral dress that has a draped, voluminous skirt. The print itself has a rather subdued palette, which works with the unexpected silhouette—imagine if the dress had a big bright print, yikes!

One thing to keep in mind: a patterned dress can look a little busy or overwhelming if not accessorized properly. Punctuate the print by adding a belt; it also will make the dress more interesting on its own. Hillary did just that by adding a slim black belt at her natural waist, which ensures that her outfit will look cute and complete even when she's not wearing a jacket. Speaking of outerwear, she picked the leather moto because the toughness of the jacket is a good fit with the flouncy dress, then finished her outfit with a simple pair of black pumps and a nude clutch. Both the shoes and the purse have cutout details, which add texture to Hillary's outfit in a subtle way.

DOG PARK

According to the results of a remarkably informal poll, most people don't think about their dog-park ensembles. We can hear it now: "Mr. Barkley doesn't care what I wear, he just wants to play fetch," or "I just want to make sure that Cookie gets her exercise; if I don't look nutso, that's enough for me." It's true that your four-legged friend is more interested in snacks than your sartorial selections—but you should still try to put a cute look together. *Your goal is to create an outfit that accounts for practical considerations (weather-appropriate, washable fabrics), while still showing some casual flair through layers or accessories.* Aim for something that has the same spirit as your Farmers Market or Errands ensembles, but even more functional.

Obviously this is not the best place to break out your favorite fancy shoes or anything high maintenance like heels; instead go for unfussy favorites like rubber galoshes or flat boots. If wearing anything other than sweatpants is unacceptable, just take a cue from Katherine's outfit and style them in a purposeful way, like tucked inside your knee-high wellies. Or you can follow Hillary's lead and go for your favorite skinny jeans; just remember that you're going to be chasing your pup around, so pick a pair with some stretch. Whatever bottoms suit you best, make sure that they're on the slim side, so you

can stuff them into your boots, or are cropped: you definitely don't want your hems dragging on the mucky ground!

The top half of your outfit obviously needs to work within certain practical parameters, but you have a little more freedom to experiment. Lightweight layers are always smart, especially if the colors and patterns play off of each other. For example, Katherine started with a red and white plaid button-down, and then added an army green canvas shirt and a black puffy vest. By choosing the vest instead of a more typical jacket, she gets to show off the nuances of her outfit and her silhouette while still staying warm. And because the vest has pockets, she doesn't have to take a handbag, which is definitely a plus.

Another easy option is to pair a voluminous top with streamlined bottoms à la Hillary. The contrast of the generously proportioned long sweater and formfitting jeans is feminine, but understated. She revved up the style factor of her basic look by accessorizing with a wide-brimmed black hat and a taupe hobo bag. The chapeau is cooler than a baseball cap, less expected than a beanie, and hides bedhead beautifully. It's also worth noting that Hillary's bag has the overall spirit of her look: slouchy and casual. A structured satchel or prim purse definitely would be an out-of-place choice for the dog park.

> " *OBVIOUSLY this is not the best place to break out your favorite fancy shoes or anything HIGH MAINTENANCE like heels.* "

OTHER OUTFIT
IDEAS

1 denim cutoffs + canvas tennis shoes + graphic tank

2 cotton dress + brown leather belt + flat sandals

3 striped long-sleeve t-shirt + slim black ankle jeans + field jacket + motorcycle boots

4 cozy sweater + cuffed jeans + moccasins

5 black leggings + rain boots + checked button-down + denim jacket or trench

GO FOR

dark colors; sturdy washable fabrics, like denim or cotton; lightweight layers; oversized sweaters; plaid work shirts; oversized button-downs; vests; cropped jeans or pants; army jackets; trench coats; flat boots or wellies; long-strap or slouchy bags; hats

STEER CLEAR

anything that needs to be dry-cleaned; bell-bottoms or other wide-leg pants or jeans; stilettos or other high heels; structured bags

RISKY BUSINESS

light-colored fabrics; skirts and dresses (no minis!); wedges

Bijou

Ruby

ENGAGEMENT PARTY

The GOAL is to create an outfit that reflects the celebratory nature of the event via FESTIVE outfit choices.

Weddings are wonderful and all, but frankly we'd rather attend an engagement party any day of the week. Why the preference for this JV event, which everyone knows is only the warm-up for the Big Day? It's way more fun! It's the party equivalent of falling in love: everything seems new and exciting and wonderful. If you're a guest, you're not sick of the betrothed couple and actually might be overjoyed that they've decided to get hitched. If you're the bride-to-be, you've yet to fight with your future partner over the registry, negotiate about the ceremony, or stress about your prospective honeymoon—in short, you're happy! Everyone's happy! That's why your goal is to create an outfit that reflects the celebratory nature of the event via festive outfit choices.

Many engagement parties are relatively dressy, which means that as an attendee, you get to break out your best party attire! Obviously you want to pick something chic—which means cocktail dresses galore—but make sure you also incorporate the "party" aspect of the evening in your outfit. You can experiment with an unexpected or of-the-moment color, glam it up in an embellished frock, or try out a more dramatic silhouette. Basically almost everything is fair game, except for anything white, cream, or even remotely bridal. It's beyond rude to do this at the wedding

and just as off-putting for the engagement party, too. As for the fiancée, obviously you're going to wear white; just make sure you find a dress that actually reflects your personal style sensibilities and is comfortable—you want to enjoy this evening!

Hillary has attended approximately 439 engagement parties, which means she's practically a professional at putting together an engagement party outfit. Whenever she opts for a little black dress, she tries to pick a unique one. In this case, she selected a strapless style with an exaggerated silhouette; after all, nothing says "party" like a peplum! As always with a LBD, you have a ton of freedom with your accessories, but one surefire idea is to go for metallics. A bronze clutch is a perfect neutral and just so happens to coordinate perfectly with Hillary's peep-toe pumps!

The future bride in this scenario—that means Katherine—kept true to her taste and picked an ultrachic body-conscious dress. The fitted sheath has a high neckline, low back, and such an interesting texture, there's nothing "traditional" about it, and she looks all the more modern for wearing it. She also used one of our favorite styling tricks: the nude shoe. Skin-tone shoes always make your legs look wildly long, which is particularly good for nights when you're going to be photographed a ton!

OTHER OUTFIT
I D E A S

1 exotic-print maxi dress + armful of gold bangles + metallic heels

2 strapless jumpsuit + nude pumps + delicate gold jewelry

3 metallic party skirt + black tank + faux fur vest

GO FOR

cocktail dresses with interesting silhouettes; bandage dresses; strapless dresses in solid colors; maxi dresses; cocktail shorts; party skirts; festive accents, like rhinestones, sequins, or embroidery; metallic accessories; nude heels

STEER CLEAR

white, ivory, cream, or anything remotely bridal (unless you're the newly engaged person!); anything too sheer, low-cut, or short; jeans and t-shirts (even if it's a casual backyard barbecue, you're there to celebrate, so step it up)

RISKY BUSINESS

red; silver (can be too close to white, so opt for a darker pewter instead); champagne (go for a darker bronze instead)

ERRANDS

If there is one thing we loathe, it's mindless casual dressing. You know what we're talking about: tracksuits, sloppy sweats, and athletic clothes worn with no intention of going to the gym. It doesn't matter if you're just running to the grocery store on the weekend or making a carpool run during the week; if you're in public you should be properly, thoughtfully dressed. Even if you spend the vast majority of your time at home (moms and freelancers, we're talking to you), you should still put a little effort into your outfit.

Besides, putting together a cute, informal outfit really isn't that much harder than pulling on your favorite elastic-waist pants, but you'll feel (and look) so

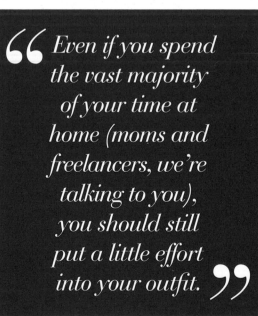

> " *Even if you spend the vast majority of your time at home (moms and freelancers, we're talking to you), you should still put a little effort into your outfit.* "

much better. The goal is to create a comfortable outfit with lightweight layers, a couple of easy accessories, and at least one tailored piece. By including that one slightly structured piece—like a khaki pant or a button-down shirt—your ensemble will have a touch of crispness, which is nice.

The key to any casual weekday outfit is to remember that the rest of the world will be in office-wear, so you should put together a look that will blend in with the rest of the corporate types.

Accessories are another way of showing you didn't just roll out of bed; just by adding a pair of sunglasses and some simple jewelry you will make your outfit so much better. Also be sure to pick a bag that fits

WEEKEND—PG. 146

OTHER OUTFIT
IDEAS

1 cozy sweater + low-slung floral skirt + flat ankle boots

2 black skinny jeans/leggings + long t-shirt + oversized cardi + gold jewelry + ballet flats

3 cropped jeans + nautical stripe long-sleeve shirt + moccasins + chic shades

4 floral dress + army jacket + oxfords

GO FOR

loose-fitting dresses; maxi skirts; full skirts; cuffed khakis; lightweight jeans; denim jackets; slim black pants; oversized button-ups; long cardigans; flannel work shirts; flat boots; moccasins; ballet flats; comfortable wedges or sandals; oxfords or loafers; printed cotton scarves

STEER CLEAR

sweats; athletic pants; sports bras; athletic shoes; flip-flops (unless you are coming from the nail salon); high heels

RISKY BUSINESS

denim shorts or skirts (on the weekend these could be spot-on, but they're a little too casual for weekday errands); leggings (go for a medium-weight pair that aren't meant for the gym!); hats (try a beret in fall and a straw fedora in warm weather)

"THE goal is to CREATE a comfortable outfit with lightweight layers, a couple of easy ACCESSORIES, and at least one TAILORED piece."

your agenda, whether that's an oversized tote (good for transporting papers) or an across-body bag (to keep your hands free during shopping). And while basic ballet flats are certainly fine, we also love lace-up shoes. Their oxford-like details nod to professional attire while remaining comfortable and cool.

Whenever Katherine has a day of errands ahead of her, she likes to wear a loose-fitting slip dress—her idea of pure comfort. To give this easy piece a little polish, she then added a slightly oversized army shirt, but there are loads of other options that would also work (like a cropped trench, shrunken blazer, or a denim button-up, vest, or jacket). To spruce up her outfit, she accessorized with a simple across-body bag, a cool pair of lace-ups with cut-out details, and a great pair of sunglasses. Sunglasses can really change the entire vibe of an outfit, so be sure to experiment with different styles to find the right fit.

While Hillary also loves easy dresses for errands, she also appreciates the power of a great pair of chinos, which is why she opted for a simple pair of khakis for her outfit. Lightweight and comfy, these pants look particularly cute when cuffed; it's just one of those little styling choices that can instantly perk up a look. Plus, these pants are just a smidge dressier than denim, making them the perfect alternative to boyfriend jeans or stretchy skinnies. Since the khakis are a bit tailored, Hillary kept the rest of her outfit—a t-shirt and an oversized striped cardi—simple. She finished the look with a foot-friendly pair of raffia wedges and an oversized black tote, two perfect touches for running errands around town.

FARMERS MARKET

The GOAL is to create an unfussy outfit that allows for temperature changes and lots of MOVEMENT.

Whether you head to the local green market every day or make a monthly appearance, it's nice to have a go-to outfit for these shopping expeditions. Plus, by perfecting your farmers market ensemble, you'll have another easy option for your casual weekend events (street fairs, brunch, antiquing, general browsing)—which is always a good thing! The goal is to create an unfussy outfit that allows for temperature changes and lots of movement. There's always the possibility you'll get dirty as you dig through produce, pick up plants, or sample something on the spot, so make sure your clothes are machine washable.

It's also important to pick a bag that is a) large enough to accommodate your layers and small impulse purchases and b) equipped with a long strap, which will keep your hands free while shopping. These trips are not always ultra-purposeful and usually include a fair amount of strolling, so pick comfortable flat shoes or sandals.

When Hillary heads to the farmers market, she typically picks one of her favorite standbys for casual weekend outfits: the shirtdress. Whether it's a

heavier, flannel shirtdress worn with leggings and motorcycle boots in the fall or a short-sleeve cotton version for spring, this is such a carefree piece for errands or shopping. She tends to favor styles with a full skirt because they're just easier to move around in and always adds a belt at her natural waist to give the simple silhouette a little more interest. Other must-takes include a thin scarf (it gives both a pop of color and can be used instead of or with a cardigan if it gets cool), sunglasses, and walking-friendly flat sandals.

Rather than reaching for velour separates—no tracksuits here!—Katherine opted for a cuffed pair of boyfriend cargos and a thin cotton button-down. By tucking in her top, she looks more polished and gets to show off one of her cute vintage belts, so feel free to do the same! While Katherine's the queen of sunglasses, for this outfit she decided to put on her brimmed panama hat. The straw chapeau is lightweight enough for a sunny day and adds some flair to her casual look. To finish her farmers market ensemble, she grabbed an across-body bag and a long-strap burlap tote and slipped on some stylish flip-flops.

OTHER OUTFIT
IDEAS

1 skinny jeans + motorcycle boots + gray jersey sweatshirt + field jacket + print scarf

2 maxi skirt + t-shirt + jean jacket + boots or sandals

3 chambray dress + straw fedora + strappy black sandals

GO FOR

WARM WEATHER: rolled khakis or baggy jeans; denim shorts; overalls; peasant skirts; loose tunics; sundresses; shirtdresses; cotton or linen button-ups; denim vests or jackets; moccasins; ballet flats; flip-flops; sandals; recyclable bags; sun hats; printed cotton scarves; oversized sunglasses

COOL WEATHER: flannel work shirts; loose cashmere sweaters; military jackets; denim jackets; sweaters with leggings; overcoats; trench coats; flat motorcycle boots; recyclable bags; wool beanies; felt fedoras

STEER CLEAR

body-conscious clothing; anything with excessive studs or metal hardware; miniskirts; bikini tops; high heels or platforms; small bags

RISKY BUSINESS

light colors; strappy tanks (beware of funky tan lines); wedges (low ones, ideally)

Fashion EVENT

While not everyone is invited to the runway shows in New York, London, Milan, and Paris, we'd be remiss if we didn't include a section on the fashion event. After all, there are opportunities galore these days, as most cities host trunk shows and other special shopping events, presentations by local designers, fashion luncheons or charity parties, meet-and-greets with established designers, and so much more. These events can lead to some serious outfit-induced anxiety, as you're going to be surrounded by stylish people who are there to celebrate (and sometimes judge) fashion.

If you're not comfortable trying out one of the latest trends or wearing something bold, you certainly can wear your favorite all-black outfit and call it a day. Chic and simple is always appropriate. However, we encourage you to take a risk with your ensemble; this is the time to try the latest looks. Accordingly, the goal is to create a fashionable outfit that includes one statement piece and one on-trend accessory.

> **" The goal is to create a *fashionable* outfit that includes one STATEMENT piece and one on-trend *accessory*. "**

When creating an outfit for a fashion event, one easy formula to follow is to start with a neutral color as the base of your outfit, then add a statement separate, such as a jacket with a directional silhouette or an impactful skirt. In the fashion world, layers and accessories are essential because they add visual interest to any look, so don't forget to include one or the other (or both!).

Also, remember to pay attention to your bag and your shoes; they can totally transform your look. An of-the-moment pair of heels or a gorgeous bag can instantly elevate an understated, basic outfit into something stylish, taking it from safe to chic in seconds.

Beauty looks are another way to easily and affordably make your ensemble ultra-current, so try a fashionable nail polish color, runway-inspired hairstyle, or a current makeup trend to add an extra kick to your overall look.

If you are attending a daytime fashion event, like a trunk show, presentation, or a luncheon,

BEAUTY BOX

A fashion event is the perfect time to try one of the season's more extreme beauty looks, so feel free to experiment with a trendier hairstyle or more dramatic makeup than usual. But be sure to only pick one major trend to try: superslick hair plus gothic eye makeup plus neon pink lips plus navy nail polish equals a big disaster.

OTHER OUTFIT
IDEAS

1 LBD + directional shoes + on-trend designer bag

2 skinny black pants + distressed gray t-shirt + sequined jacket

3 pencil skirt + semi-sheer button-up + cropped leather moto jacket

4 boyfriend blazer + silk tank/tunic + leather leggings

5 leather skirt + crisp button-up + rhinestone jewelry

"*You can certainly wear your favorite all-black outfit and call it a day. CHIC and SIMPLE is always appropriate.*"

this is an excellent time to play with a bold color or pattern. As mentioned earlier, Hillary started with a neutral base—a sleeveless nude blouse—then added a vivid yellow silk-chiffon skirt as her statement piece. Again, this is always a good time to pick playful accessories, so she added a beaded, striped belt and yellow snake print heels for extra flair. The finishing touches come courtesy of a cream-colored classic bag with a ladylike shape, another neutral touch that balances the dramatic tones in her look.

> *"An OF-THE-MOMENT pair of heels or a gorgeous bag can instantly ELEVATE an understated, basic outfit into something stylish, taking it from safe to chic in seconds."*

When you have a fashion show or some other nighttime event to attend, make an impact by opting for texture and sparkle instead of color or prints. For example, Katherine built her look around an amazing silver sequined skirt, paired with a simple red v-neck t-shirt for a fabulous high/low mix. To tone down the inherent fanciness of the sparkly skirt, she added a shrunken denim jacket and then threw on her go-to favorite leather jacket.

In addition to the fact that the double layers make the whole outfit so much more interesting, Katherine knows she always gets compliments on that jacket, which gives her the confidence to carry off this bold look. She accessorized with an excellent, understated clutch and some simple black ankle boots, which wisely keeps the focus on her thoughtfully chosen outfit.

ACCESSORY ESSENTIAL

FASHIONABLE FOOTWEAR

One incredibly easy way to perfect and elevate your fashion event outfit is to add a pair of au courant shoes. By accessorizing with statement heels or a runway-inspired pair of ankle boots, you'll look relevant and chic—even if you're just wearing an LBD.

GO FOR

all-black outfits; a pop of color or sequins; leather; directional separates; layered tops and jackets; dramatic skirts; of-the-moment pants; faux fur jackets and vests; statement jewelry; animal-print accents; on-trend beauty, like a bold nail polish

STEER CLEAR

excessive or prominent logo prints; wrinkles (make sure you steam or iron before you go); too many trends at once; scuffed shoes; chipped mani/pedi

RISKY BUSINESS

bright colors (great for day, less so for night); bold graphic prints; denim (the jean du jour can be spot-on if worn with something dressier, like sequins or leather; when in doubt, choose a dark wash); hats (a hat is a hindrance in a large crowd)

GAME NIGHT

The GOAL is to create an outfit that has a little polish, but is also casual enough that YOU could sit on the floor.

The game itself is irrelevant—it could be poker or pai gow, Scrabble or charades, bunco or back-gammon—but what you wear while playing is always important! After all, even if you lose the round or have to fold your hand, when you look great, you'll always feel like a winner.

When attending a game night, it probably goes without saying that you need to be comfort-able, but that doesn't mean you should look like one of the sloppy pros playing Texas Hold'em on ESPN. (Ew!) The goal is to create an outfit that has a little polish, but is also casual enough that you could sit on the floor. The look should be somewhat similar to what you'd wear to a Dinner Party at someone's house, but even more relaxed.

When creating your game night ensemble, it's always a good idea to start with a great pair of pants, preferably either a loose-fit style or some-thing with stretch. If you loathe pants for some reason, a full or floor-length skirt could also work, as would a maxi dress; just make sure you add cot-ton or denim layers to keep things casual. Re-member, you're probably going to be sitting for the majority of the evening, so make sure that whatever you pick doesn't cut, chafe, or bind; you want to keep your focus on the competition at hand, not your pants.

Also, this is yet another great occasion for light-weight layers (aren't they all?), for both practical and sartorial purposes. There are so many options to pick from—cardigans, vests, bed jackets—that it's easy to find the perfect piece for your personal style. Additionally, we usually recommend wear-ing slip-on shoes; they're an unfussy choice, plus some hostesses insist on leaving your footwear at the door, so it's nice not to have to worry about undoing a million buckles.

While no one would call us card sharks, we do have some sharp outfits for any type of game-playing situation. Hillary picked her favorite black skinny jeans as the base of her look; they're an accommodating choice, thanks to their super-stretchy material. Katherine opted for a relaxed pair of print pants, which she cuffed to show off her cute bow-bedecked flats. Since her trousers are the focus of the look, she kept the rest of her outfit neutral via a simple t-shirt and a short-sleeve cardigan sweater.

Hillary also opted for a basic tee, but she then added a gorgeous peacock-print draped kimono to liven up her outfit. Though the satiny material is definitely a little dressy, its billowy silhouette gives it more of a slouchy boudoir effect, which feels appropriate for this occasion. It's really the perfect cover-up for any outfit, as it adds a great deal of style with very little effort. As for the rest of our looks, everything's pretty simple, but feel free to wear a fun piece of costume jewelry (ideally a ring or bracelet) if you want.

OTHER OUTFIT
IDEAS

1 graphic tee + sparkly cardigan + skinny jeans + flats

2 oversized leopard-print sweater + leggings + flats

3 black romper + cropped trench coat + clogs

4 cuffed slouchy jeans + loafers + striped sweater

5 black cotton/stretch maxi skirt + thin tank + denim jacket

GO FOR

chunky knits; skinny jeans with stretch; relaxed trousers; boyfriend pants; cropped pants; kimonos; bed jackets; vests; cardigans; simple t-shirts; easy maxi skirts or dresses; cashmere pullovers; full skirts; slip-on flats or sandals; one fun piece of costume jewelry; natural hair and makeup

STEER CLEAR

anything tight or uncomfortable; workwear; formal outfits; miniskirts; strappy/complicated shoes; heavy makeup; fancy hair

RISKY BUSINESS

perishable fabrics; linen pants; tailored jackets

GIRLS'
NIGHT OUT

The GOAL is to create an outfit that makes you feel ULTRA-CONFIDENT; extra points for including an outrageous, on-trend piece or FASHION-forward accent.

And now we come to what might be the most fun social situation in this book—Girls' Night Out! As you no doubt know, the Girls' Night Out, or GNO as we like to call it, is all about going out and getting crazy with your friends, so it's really the perfect time to try something daring and create an inspired, of-the-moment look. That means breaking out your most outrageous party dress, a new pair of directional heels, or a runway-inspired neon eyeliner look—whatever makes you feel au courant and cool. The goal is to create an outfit that makes you feel ultra-confident; extra points for including an outrageous, on-trend piece or fashion-forward accent.

There is no social occasion that is more fitting for a little fashion experimentation than the GNO, so please use this evening to try something fresh, take a style or beauty risk, and create an innovative look. That said, there is one thing we simply

BEAUTY BOX

A GNO is the perfect time to test-drive an edgy beauty look. For example, try the season's most daring lip color, whether that's a bright red, electric pink, or rich wine. Want to experiment with neon eyeliner, a strong brow, or intense eyelashes? Do it! Is there a hairstyle you're curious about, like an ultra-deep side part, huge bouncy curls, or super-straight and slick locks? Experiment! The GNO is also the ideal occasion to play with hair accessories, so bust out your best headbands and cool clip-ins.

GO FOR

mini dresses in vibrant colors; leather shorts, skirts, or pants; dress shorts with or without tights; faux fur vests or jackets; platform heels; statement accessories like a chunky necklace, big earrings, or a wrist of bangles; animal-print accents like leopard ankle boots; oversized clutches; the season's coolest beauty trend

STEER CLEAR

anything baggy; modest necklines; corporate clothes; baby doll or empire-waist dresses and tops; maxi skirts or dresses; flats (unless you are very pregnant!); day bags

RISKY BUSINESS

jeans (if you must, go for black or gray and make sure they are tight; otherwise please try something new); menswear or workwear

STYLE SUGGESTION

If you're generally more conservative when it comes to your wardrobe, show your spirit through your shoes and bags. Maybe you wouldn't wear a sequined dress or a neon pink skirt, but you can interpret these bold trends in smaller doses.

OTHER OUTFIT IDEAS

1. leather skirt + distressed concert tee + bright platforms

2. sparkly mini + solid semi-sheer tank + shrunken denim jacket

3. draped tank + body-conscious skirt + lace-up ankle boots

4. LBD + red lip + studded heels + leopard coat

5. print pants + low-cut top + strappy heel

> ## *"The GNO is also the perfect time to try something fresh, take a risk, and really experiment with your look."*

cannot recommend or condone wearing on a GNO: jeans. Yes, we know you love your jeans and you can't live without them, but seriously ladies: put them away for a night. It's a little lazy, especially when you consider how many other amazing options are available. Need suggestions? How about a body-con dress, silky or sequined shorts, leather leggings, a fancy jumpsuit, a short flippy skirt—the list goes on and on. Our point is this: style-wise, you can do so much better than jeans, so please step outside your wardrobe box and step it up a notch or two (or three!).

If you need a little help figuring out your GNO outfit—everyone does at some point!—one easy way to get a little inspiration is to look to your favorite runway shows and celebrity ensembles. You're bound to stumble across an outfit that you like or at least one that will spark an idea for an even better look! Conversely, sometimes it's easier to start with what you already have in your closet. One trick we often use is taking a trendy new piece and styling it with one of our favorite wardrobe staples (like a perfect semi-sheer gray t-shirt or a seasonless black miniskirt). The combination of classic and au courant is always excellent—especially when worn with a killer pair of heels!

On that note, let's talk about the perfect GNO accessories. If your friends are anything like our friends, a night out involves lots of dancing, so make sure that your heels are not only hot, but comfortable, too. You don't want to be the girl whose blisters are keeping her from killing it on the dance floor, right? As for your bag, make sure you pick something that's specifically appropriate for nighttime; in other words, leave the work tote at home! So what style should you pick? If you're a responsible human, go for a clutch; otherwise, for the crazy ladies, try a long-strap bag (like Hillary did for her outfit). Our recommendation is to wear it across your body, as this will ensure you don't leave it in the bar, club, or cab accidentally.

While Katherine often goes for an LBD and a strong red lip for her nights on the town, she also experiments with statement colors, as you can see from her outfit. She opted for a vibrant yellow miniskirt as the foundation of her outfit—a piece she'd typically wear with a draped white T-shirt and a leather jacket—paired with a lingerie-inspired corset top. Both pieces allow her to move freely, a necessity when dancing! Hillary typically opts for some sort of short and flouncy skirt for her GNOs, but this time around she picked a figure-hugging frock in a pretty violet-blue hue. Finishing touches come from a pair of snake print pumps and some fuchsia lipstick—always a fun choice for a GNO.

gRADUATION

The GOAL is to create an outfit that's slightly dressy, conducive to sitting, and can take you from EARLY morning festivities to late afternoon.

Cue "Pomp and Circumstance," dear readers, because it's time to discuss that oh-so-joyous occasion—Graduation Day! Okay, let's be honest: it's definitely an important day, but it's also an extremely long day that often involves sitting outside for prolonged periods of time. Plus, depending on the place of higher learning, this usually means hours in the sweltering sun—a time period that feels even hotter if you're the graduate and wearing a heavy robe over your outfit. The goal is to create an outfit that's slightly dressy, conducive to sitting, and can take you from early morning activities through late afternoon festivities.

When constructing your graduation outfit, be sure to consider the time of year—late spring/early summer—which means you should stick to primarily light-colored, lightweight fabrics. Breathable fabrics are your friend for this social situation, but please refrain from picking any fussy materials (silk, we mean you) because heat + sitting = wrinkles. Your footwear is also of paramount importance; there's always a tremendous amount of walking on the graduation day agenda, so make sure your chosen shoes are up to the task. Your outfit should be a bit demure, as this is a family event, so your best bet is to pick a dress: it's light, airy, and a traditional choice. Last, but certainly not least, you need to remember to wear sunscreen!

On these diploma days, Hillary always goes for a dress. While a strapless or spaghetti-strap dress is definitely appropriate, to avoid potential strap marks altogether, she selected a dress with short, wide sleeves instead. (Large armholes are a savvy choice for sweltering days, as they ensure you'll never see sweat marks.) The dress's lightweight fabric and draped shape are perfect for this sort of situation, and the addition of a wide belt at her natural waist adds a little polish to the look. Hillary picked a simple pair of tan wedges—always easy to walk in—for this occasion and finished the ensemble with a cute cork clutch, perfect for a summer daytime outfit.

To give you another silhouette to consider, Katherine went for separates and combined a soft, sleeveless button-up blouse and a soft pair of drawstring pants for her graduation look. With the foundation of her outfit set, she then added a long linen jacket in a faded leopard print. Admittedly, linen can be tricky—it wrinkles easily—but it works with the jacket's deconstructed style. Since her outfit is relatively neutral, Katherine added a bright pair of peep-toe heels for a pop of color and accessorized with a chic wire-frame sunglasses. The frames are super-lightweight, always a good thing when wearing them for hours on end!

OTHER OUTFIT IDEAS

1 pencil skirt + sleeveless button-up blouse + nude pumps + ladylike bag

2 white sundress + brown leather waist belt + raffia clutch + red sandals

3 chiffon maxi dress + flat strappy sandals + oversized sunglasses

GO FOR

light colors; cotton or other summery materials; short-sleeve, spaghetti-strap, or strapless dresses; wedges; medium-sized day bags or totes; casual clutches; natural makeup; chic sunglasses

STEER CLEAR

fabrics that wrinkle easily; long-sleeve blouses that will show perspiration; full skirts if you're the graduate (it will make you look larger than you are underneath your robe!); jeans

RISKY BUSINESS

black (if you must, make sure you pick lightweight, sheer fabrics); strapless dresses (you don't want to show too much skin, so go for a loose fit and a mid-to-maxi length and bring a light wrap); hats (though they are great for sun protection, some styles will block other people's view, so make sure you pick a compact style)

CONSERVATIVE Job INTERVIEW

When considering any stressful event—taking a test, making a wedding speech, heck, even flying—we like to stack the decks in our favor. Being properly prepared is really the best way to succeed in most high-pressure situations, which is why putting together the perfect job-interview outfit is so important. You can't dictate how the interview itself goes, but there are a few things you can control, namely what you're wearing.

When applying for jobs in more conservative fields, there are a number of rules to follow, but that doesn't mean you're doomed to a life of dull dressing. The goal is to create a classic, polished outfit that shows your professionalism and good taste. Remember to check the company's dress code before you go and wear something that errs on the most formal side of their wardrobe spectrum. When in doubt, it's always a smart choice to take the most conservative route.

When preparing your interview outfit, don't waste your time trying to reinvent the wheel. Stick to sober neutrals, such as black, navy, or gray, and make sure that everything you're wearing is in tip-top shape. Yes, obsess over the details, and remember: the perfect fit is of paramount importance.

Now, this doesn't mean you need to buy an ultraexpensive designer suit; however, you should make sure that everything, from the hems to the cuffs, fits you flawlessly. We suggest taking a trip to the tailor with your suit for any necessary adjustments—trust us, it's worth it.

Other things to consider are your shoes and bag: make sure both are in completely impeccable condition and appropriate. Closed-toe heels are definitely always an appropriate choice and peep-toe

> *"The goal is to create a CLASSIC, polished outfit that shows your professionalism and good taste."*

OTHER OUTFIT IDEAS

1. gray pencil skirt + silky shell + black blazer + vintage bracelet

2. black wide-leg pants + crisp button-up blouse + cropped gray blazer + interesting belt

3. knee-length fitted dress + chic suit jacket + structured satchel + oversized pearl studs

4. slim navy suit + white blouse + skinny belt with gold buckle

5. taupe knee-length skirt + khaki silk blouse + nude pumps

HILLARY

MORE CONSERVATIVE OPTIONS:
Replace tapered pants with a classic wide-leg pair or straight-leg trousers. Instead of a print blouse, substitute a crisp, classic button-up in a solid, neutral color like white or blue. If you're interviewing in the most traditional fields—law, banking, business—opt for a skirt instead of pants, preferably something slim and to the knee.

HOW TO
BUY A SUIT

A good rule of thumb is to buy the suit pants based on how they fit your largest area, and then tailor the other areas accordingly. Remember, it's always better to buy something a little big and have it fitted exactly to your frame; squeezing into a suit that's a little too small is not very chic.

GO FOR

suits that fit your body perfectly in a dark neutral color (charcoal or black is best); silky blouses with feminine details; crisp clean button-ups; silk tanks (always worn with a jacket); one interesting accessory, like a men's watch; closed or peep-toe shoes with a modest heel in a dark color

STEER CLEAR

anything sheer; sleeveless tops with no jacket; body-con dresses or skirts; miniskirts; maxi skirts or dresses; full skirts or dresses; ill-fitting suits; worn-out shoes; flats; open-toed shoes; casual bags; dark eye makeup; red lipstick

RISKY BUSINESS

dresses (dresses work great under a blazer as long as the length is modest—to the knee—and they aren't body conscious); supersized statement jewelry

KATHERINE

MORE CONSERVATIVE OPTIONS: Instead of a print skirt, pick a solid color, such as black or gray. Exchange the white bag for a dark neutral and opt for a more subtle heel.

" *WHEN in doubt, it's always a smart choice to take the most* CONSERVATIVE *route.* "

styles can be fine, too, but they are considered slightly less conservative. As for your bag, we think a structured purse is the best choice, and ideally it should be big enough to hold your portfolio.

That said, there are plenty of ways to spice up a workwear ensemble and embrace your personal style on the (conservative) job. If you feel that your prospective employer is more traditional, check out More Conservative Options for our suggestions on how to make these ensembles even more corporate.

For example, Hillary decided to go for a pantsuit for this situation, but rather than wearing a traditional silhouette, she picked a jacket with a slightly strong shoulder and a pair of tapered pants. By choosing the tapered trousers she not only gets to show off her shoes—a classic pair of gray pumps—she also reveals her style in a very chic way. Instead of wearing a traditional blouse, she went for a subtle print worn over a fitted black tank. The combination of the suit's unexpected silhouette and the nonblack accessories ensures

this outfit is not only chic, it's also totally appropriate for the occasion.

Katherine's conservative job interview outfit also shows she thinks outside of the corporate box, but still knows how to play by the rules—always a good thing to communicate! She decided to wear a print pencil skirt from one of her favorite suits, but instead of pairing it with the matching jacket, she selected a solid-colored lightweight blazer. The jacket has a large lapel, so Katherine belted it to amplify the style factor of this outfit. To balance out this trendy trick, she went with a totally classic ivory blouse, which she buttoned up completely for a modest touch.

While there's no ironclad rule about hosiery, since her skirt is above the knee, she added a pair of opaque tights and completed her outfit with some sleek black pumps. The finishing touch: a large, professional bag in a conservative style and an unexpected color. The shape says "I take my work home with me," but the light color is a chic choice.

J CREATIVE

Job
INTERVIEW

THE GOAL is to create an outfit that combines one classic suit element with a piece that communicates your CREATIVITY.

Unlike an interview for a conservative job, when you're applying for a position in a creative field—advertising, public relations, production, art, entertainment—you have a bit more leeway. Your ensemble can be a little less formal (you don't have to wear a suit, or even a jacket necessarily); it should express your sensibilities (in this environment, personality is a plus, not a flaw); and it needs to be super-sharp, as you will be judged on your style (it's another way of showing your taste level).

The goal is to create an outfit that combines one classic suit element with a piece that communicates your creativity. The recipe is simple: mix one neutral-colored corporate item, like a blazer, pencil skirt, or pair of slacks, with something that reveals your fashion point of view, like a graphic-print blouse, statement belt, or a couple of statement accessories.

Though it probably goes without saying, please leave the jeans at home; sure, future bosses might

be wearing them, but they already have their jobs. Plus, being slightly overdressed is a sign of respect, something your potential employer will no doubt appreciate. While we advise against most colors or bold prints for the Conservative Job Interview, feel free to use them—judiciously—in this situation. A vibrant blouse with a classic cut or a traditional bag in an unexpected print can be fabulous for the Creative Job Interview.

While there are almost limitless possibilities for the Creative Job Interview outfit, we put together two suggestions for you to use as jumping-off points. Katherine went for a pair of tapered trousers in olive green wool; the carrot shape is a bit more directional, and it allows her to spotlight a wonderful, double-wrap belt and a cool pair of peep-toe pumps.

As an alternative to a blouse, she opted for a black long-sleeve bodysuit with a modest neckline, to balance out the top's tight fit. To add more interest to her outfit, she chose two unique

STYLE
SUGGESTION

In addition to showing your personality and taste level by accessorizing with your favorite bracelet or a statement watch, a belt can be another key accent piece. Use a belt in a contrasting color to add interest to a monochromatic ensemble or a dark neutral to ground a print top; either way, belts add polish!

HOW TO

SPICE UP A BASIC SUIT

Say you have two suits: one black (fitted blazer, wide-leg trousers) and one gray (pencil skirt; shrunken jacket). Rather than wearing them as is, it's always more interesting to mix and match. Try gray pencil skirt with the black blazer and a silky blouse or shell. Or you could wear the black trousers with the gray blazer, paired with a crisp button-up. Just make sure you add one interesting accessory that shows off your style, like a vintage bracelet, chunky choker, or classic pearls.

" *THE RECIPE IS SIMPLE: mix one neutral-colored corporate item, like a BLAZER, pencil skirt, or PAIR OF slacks, with something that reveals your FASHION POINT OF VIEW.* "

OTHER OUTFIT IDEAS

1 pencil skirt + tucked-in blouse + stacked bangles/statement necklace + bright belt

2 print shell + cardigan + slim skirt + colorful heels

3 wide-leg trousers + tucked-in t-shirt + cropped blazer + chunky chains

GO FOR

slim black pants; carrot trousers; wide-leg slacks; 7/8 pants; solid-colored knee-length dresses; colorful or graphic-print blouses; sheer blouses with camisoles underneath; colorful heels (closed or peep-toe); ankle boots with a heel or wedge; small animal-print accents, like a leopard-print belt or pumps

STEER CLEAR

jeans; denim skirts or jackets; strapless tops; maxi dresses or skirts; sandals or flats; hats (even if you're interviewing at Vogue and berets are the latest trend—never wear a hat to a job interview)

RISKY BUSINESS

tank tops (are great, but you still need to wear something over your shoulders—even if it is hot outside!); bold lipstick (it's too distracting, so go for a stain instead)

> *"Being slightly overdressed is a sign of respect, something your potential employer will no doubt appreciate."*

accessories: a beaded statement necklace and a purple and gray leopard-print satchel.

Hillary decided to show her style through a bright floral blouse, but then balanced it for business by adding classic black accents. Since her top is a little intense, she decided to break up the pattern by accessorizing with a wide black belt at her natural waist; this gives some polish to the look and tempers the top's boldness.

To finish the look, Hillary opted for a simple black pencil skirt, peep-toe pumps, and a structured black leather tote. The resulting outfit is pulled together but packed with personality—just the sort of balance you need in this situation.

BEAUTY BOX

Above all else, you want to look professional, so make sure your beauty look reflects this too. Don't forget to get a manicure before your interview; we like natural, clean, buffed nails or a simple nude polish best.

KIDS' EVENT

The GOAL is to create an outfit that allows you to partake in ALL the day's ACTIVITIES and can withstand dirty hands, frosting, and grass stains.

While all of us have attended a number of Kids' Events and know exactly what goes on at such a soiree—cake, games, party favors—it's possible you haven't been to one as an adult! If you don't have kids and/or have very little experience with them, getting invited to a child's party can lead to some sartorial queries. When we were five, parties meant an opportunity to wear things like costumes, overalls, and crinoline skirts—but that is definitely not going to cut it now. Most Kids' Events involve lots of activities, very few chairs, and movement galore, so when you're putting an outfit together, take all of those facts into consideration.

If you're like us and so used to wearing heels that it's hard to go without them, opt for a comfortable pair of wedges; otherwise stick to flats, sandals, or simple sneakers. Also remember that it's a family event, so don't wear anything too revealing. If you do decide to go for a skirt, make sure it's either full or maxi, so that you will be able to sit cross-legged if you want. Generally speaking, you should stay away from dark colors and go for light or bright instead; you'll seem more approachable to the little ones—and their parents—if you don't look like a member of the Insane Clown Posse.

If there's ever an appropriate time for a play-suit or romper, a Kids' Event is definitely it. As such, Katherine picked a light denim button-up version, which she wore over a muted print button-up. The layered look is not only cute and visually intriguing, it also adds warmth so she doesn't need a sweater. Since she kept her jewelry minimal—toddlers tend to tug at necklaces and earrings, ouch!—she added a belt to her outfit, which coordinates perfectly with her brown leather platforms. Again, layers always add interest to an outfit, so she accessorized with a pair of socks and threw on a large bag with a long strap, which can be worn on the shoulder or across the body.

The hands-free factor of the across-body bag is huge for the Kids' Event, which is why Hillary picked one, too! In addition to the practical purse, she selected a stretchy pair of thin corduroy pants as the base of her look, and then added a soft print tank and a long caramel-colored cardigan over it. Her lightweight layers are all slightly fitted, which means she can move freely all day long—a necessity when hitting piñatas and playing Pin the Tail on the Donkey!

OTHER OUTFIT IDEAS

1 t-shirt + denim vest/ jacket + full floral skirt + moccasins

2 cuffed denim shorts + tank top + kimono jacket

3 soft maxi dress + cardigan + flat sandals

4 bell-bottom/flare jeans + tucked-in t-shirt + wedges

5 denim boyfriend shorts + nautical stripe tank + army jacket + oxfords

GO FOR

jeans; shorts; playsuits or jumpsuits; corduroys; rolled khakis or cargo pants; machine-washable button-ups; tank tops and cardigans; maxi dresses; long-sleeve t-shirts; lightweight outerwear like cardigans, cropped trenches, or army jackets; wedges or flat sandals; flat boots or moccasins

STEER CLEAR

all-black outfits (or other dark colors); silk, lace, or other perishable fabrics; anything with studs or heavy hardware; mini- or pencil skirts; body-conscious dresses; workwear; sweats; high-heeled boots or shoes

RISKY BUSINESS

skirts (go for full skirts that are at least to the knee in order to sit on the ground)

...... Riley

LADIES' LUNCHEON

Technically we're calling this situation the Ladies' Luncheon, but don't let the name fool you. The type of outfit this occasion calls for is really multipurpose and can also be used for a bridal or baby shower, birthday or charity luncheon, or even an afternoon tea party. When creating your look, remember that this event is definitely female-centric, which means a) you need to look somewhat ladylike, and b) you can be a bit more fashion-forward because most women appreciate the more experimental aspects of fashion. *The goal is to create a modest outfit that's more festive than what you'd wear to work or a daytime religious occasion, but less casual than a cocktail party look.* Remember to pay attention to the lunch's location—is it at a private home or a four-star restaurant?—and use that to inform your wardrobe selection. Some establishments have a dress code (as we discussed in Country Club), so it's worth doing a little research before creating the perfect look.

Generally speaking, the most appropriate choices for a Ladies' Luncheon are dresses or skirts, though you can opt for a nice pair of pants—but skip the jeans. Also, remember that not everyone in attendance will be in your age bracket, so always go for the most respectful version of your outfit. You don't want to give anyone reason to talk about your personal style in a negative way, so stay away from short, tight, and low-cut garments. Pay attention to your grooming, too—women always notice these types of details—so your mani/pedi should be perfect, hair look polished, and makeup light.

Additionally, please remember to not outdo your hostess/the guest of honor. If it's someone's special day, like a birthday or a baby shower, let her shine by not wearing your most over-the-top outfit. If it's a bridal shower, let the bride-to-be wear white.

The Ladies' Luncheon is also an opportunity to embrace and celebrate your feminine side and go for something girly. For example, Katherine picked a light pink striped blazer for this occasion—a color she almost never wears—as it's the perfect shade for this sort of event. Since she's a fan of mixing prints, she wore the jacket with a short-sleeve polka-dot silk dress with a knee-length hem. Since the LL is literally all about the ladies, she picked a structured, chic ivory purse just big enough to hold the essentials: tortoiseshell sunglasses, lip gloss, and wallet. Finishing touches come via a perfect pair of nude pumps and gold heart earrings, which will be clearly seen since her hair is pinned back off her face.

Hillary put together a similarly polished ensemble, created by combining a few timeless pieces with some youthful dashes of color. She started her outfit with a classic, crisp, white button-up blouse and then livened up her look with a bright print pencil skirt. Though the skirt is definitely a statement print, the simple silhouette really balances it out. To accessorize her outfit, Hillary opted for a yellow and gold vintage bracelet—a personal touch—and some smart peep-toe pumps. Last, but certainly not least, she grabbed a pale trench coat, which is her go-to lightweight outerwear option.

OTHER OUTFIT
IDEAS

1 floral dress + cropped trench + lace-up booties

2 silky tapered trousers + feminine shell/tank + statement necklace

3 lace knee-length dress + black pumps + vibrant lip color

4 tiered skirt + silk shell + cropped blazer

GO FOR

feminine dresses and blouses; full skater skirts; pencil skirts; maxi skirts and dresses; carrot trousers or wide-leg slacks; trench coats or cardigans; fitted blazers in a girly color; nude pumps; peep-toe or open-toe heels; ladylike structured or quilted handbags; bright accessories

STEER CLEAR

anything too short; any fabric that will wrinkle badly (you'll be sitting for a long time); sequins; linen pants; body-con dresses and skirts; jeans; heavy makeup; chipped nails; dirty hair

RISKY BUSINESS

leather; sheer skirts, tops, and dresses; denim vests or jackets (balance these pieces with something fancier—also they may be a no-no given some dress codes); flats (most women will likely be in heels)

MEET the PARENTS

The GOAL is to create a respectful and feminine outfit that still remains TRUE to your personal taste.

It doesn't matter if you're fifteen or fifty; meeting your beau's parents is a nerve-racking situation. The fact of the matter is, you like this person a great deal and you want his folks to approve of you—which hopefully they will—so why not boost your odds of that happening and show up in a perfectly appointed outfit? If they're already predisposed to liking you, a thoughtfully chosen ensemble will only solidify their acceptance. Conversely, if you're about to meet two overprotective parental units who are terribly critical of anyone their child brings home, it's really imperative that you look appropriate.

The goal is to create a respectful and feminine outfit that still remains true to your personal taste.

Generally speaking, it's a good idea to shoot for something that's a bit more conservative than what you'd wear on a First Date, but not as dressy as what you'd pick for a Daytime Religious Occasion.

> *"It's a good idea to shoot for something that's a bit more conservative than what you'd wear on a First Date."*

When assembling said outfit, there are a few things you should take into consideration to make sure you ace this situation. It's always a good idea to equip yourself with information, so start by asking your boyfriend to describe his parents. Knowing that they're extremely conservative, semi-traditional, or completely casual will give you a great jumping-off point when determining how to style your ensemble.

Whatever you pick, make sure that you're comfortable—meaning you can easily sit, stand, and

BEAUTY BOX

When meeting the folks, make sure your beauty look is correct for the occasion. Just like on a First Date, you should go for a polished, groomed look that doesn't require loads of makeup. A lipstain in a natural color is a great idea (no fear of getting lipstick on your teeth!) and we suggest getting a mani with classic pinky-nude polish, too.

OTHER OUTFIT IDEAS

1. sundress + cardigan + espadrilles

2. navy trousers + cream blouse + sparkly cardigan + nude pumps

3. khaki skirt + brown leather belt + embellished tank + denim jacket

4. long-sleeve mini-dress + opaque tights + embellished flats

5. floral dress + brown leather jacket + gray pumps

STYLE SUGGESTION

If the first meeting is taking place at your beau's home, flats might be the right choice. Of course this depends on the time of day and how formal the family is; for example, if you're going over for a weekend brunch, flats would be great and will keep his mom from feeling underdressed.

GO FOR

full skirts (nothing too short); subtle print dresses; colorful shift dresses; girly blouses; smart jackets; striped tops; slim black pants; smart shoes (see the Job Interview sections for more suggestions); personal accessories; opaque tights

STEER CLEAR

leather; anything with extreme studs or embellishments; anything super-sheer, tight, short, or revealing; strapless dresses; body-con skirts and dresses; club shoes; lace or fishnet tights

RISKY BUSINESS

jeans (opt for semi-fitted medium-to-dark washed denim in a classic cut); boots (nothing over the knee or with an extreme platform or heel—that feels too sexy—stay with something ankle or below the knee, either flat, wedge, or a modest heel)

"Jeans are a TRICKY pick for meeting the parents, but they CAN WORK, if worn correctly."

walk—because fidgeting with your clothes is definitely a no-no. It's also important to remain true to who you are in your wardrobe selections. Ideally you'll be seeing much more of his parents, so you don't want to present yourself in an incorrect way.

For the most part, jeans are a tricky pick for meeting the parents, but they can work if worn correctly, as Katherine shows. If you want to wear denim, make sure you stay away from slouchy shapes (like boyfriend jeans) or distressed styles (no matter how popular they might be) altogether. Instead, take a cue from Katherine and go for a fitted, flattering pair of jeans in a solid, medium-blue wash. She picked a slightly flared silhouette, but you should select whatever style works best on your body.

To tidy up her look, Katherine balanced her formfitting jeans with a modest, girly blouse: the long sleeves and prim neckline are respectful choices. Shoe-wise, she selected brown wedges, which are easy to walk in, but give her a little height, which is more formal than flats and dresses up the denim.

If you'd prefer to wear something that is a bit more dressed up, it's always a good idea to go with a skirt à la Hillary. She picked a full skirt with a floral print as the foundation of her look, and then added a long-sleeve, bow-tie silk blouse and a fitted blazer. The mixed prints show a little personality, but of course, you could swap either piece out for a solid iteration, too. Since her outfit is so colorful, she balanced all of the brightness with a foot-friendly pair of nude platform pumps and a neutral tote. The finishing touch: a classic, multi-hued jeweled bracelet.

MUSIC FESTIVAL

The GOAL is to create an outfit that works in challenging weather and is incredibly comfortable, but is still infused with COOLNESS.

No matter if you're a Coachella fanatic or a Lollapalooza lover, a Glastonbury girl or a Bonnaroo buff, is there anything more amazing than a summer music festival? Only if you don't like seeing your favorite bands and musicians, despise the collective camaraderie experienced at such gatherings, and loathe the invariably interesting fashion statements you can see at these shows! Call us crazy, consider us presumptuous, but we have a feeling that's not you, dear reader.

Assuming you attend such fests, let's talk about what you wear: an all-day music festival is the perfect time to embrace your inner bohemian. The goal is to create an outfit that works

> 66 *When in doubt about what to wear, always look to the patron style saints of music festivals: Kate Moss, Sienna Miller, and Nicole Richie.* 99

in challenging weather and is incredibly comfortable, but is still infused with coolness. When in doubt about what to wear, always look to the patron style saints of music festivals: Kate Moss, Sienna Miller, and Nicole Richie.

Of all the many things you need to think about when creating your fashionable fest ensemble, remember that your look needs to be incredibly versatile. You'll probably be out from morning till after midnight, so it's imperative that your outfit is in sync with the forecast. Also, since most music festivals are held in fields—which means grass, dust, and mud—you need to pick hardy fabrics that won't be immediately ru-

ined by the elements. Denim is always a good choice, as are darker neutrals and busy or bold print pieces; basically you want something that will allow you to sit on the ground and won't show dirt immediately. Always go for a shoe style that is conducive to standing and walking (flats), and make sure that they're properly broken in.

Accessory-wise, it's always a smart idea to bring a sun hat, large sunglasses, and an over-sized lightweight scarf, which you can use as a post-sunset cover-up or as a picnic blanket. And, just as we discussed for a Concert, go for a bag with a long strap so that you can wear it across your body.

As an enthusiastic music festival attendee, Hillary has been working on her "uniform" for a number of years. While there are slight variations, the foundation piece is usually the same: a long, full maxi dress. This time she picked an ultralightweight cotton version with a large, neutral print; though it's voluminous, the fabric is really airy, so she won't overheat.

To avoid looking like a tent, she added a braided leather belt at her natural waist, then completed the ensemble with flat flip-flops, a long-strap bag accessorized with a summer scarf, and a wide-brimmed hat.

Katherine wanted a look that was boho-glam, so she started with her favorite Levi's cutoffs and paired them with an embellished tank. Assuming the weather report calls for rain, she'd go for a pair of black rubber rain boots, as shown; otherwise she'd sub in a pair of of-the-moment sandals.

To further combat the rain, she added an oversized poncho that would cover her entire outfit, if need be. It's a smart choice for outer-wear: it's light, so she can easily pack it in her bag, plus it would make a perfect waterproof ground covering! On that note, when determining which bag to take, make sure it's not heavy (you'll be carrying it all day, remember?) and that you can easily fit all your essentials inside.

BEAUTY BOX

A music festival is challenging because you need to come up with a beauty look that lasts all day and in various temperatures. Be sure to protect your skin: use a high SPF liquid sunscreen for your face and tinted moisturizer with SPF or mineral powder on your t-zone. Braids or messy updos are perfect for this situation, too; just make sure you protect your part from the sun!

OTHER OUTFIT IDEAS

1. maxi skirt + semi-sheer tank + low-slung belt + sandals
2. cutoffs + flat suede ankle boots + tie-dye tank
3. floral-print dress + woven sandals + across-body bag
4. chambray dress + black sandals + straw fedora
5. black shorts + fringe vest + bucket bag

STYLE SUGGESTION

Most music festivals involve sun, so make sure you don't wear anything—shoes, tops, dresses, whatever—with crazy straps. The tan lines will haunt you for ages; it's not a pretty sight. Whatever you wear, just make sure you load up on sunscreen before you go!

GO FOR

bohemian print maxi dresses and skirts; strapless tops and dresses; tank tops; breezy tops; denim cutoffs; full-skirted sundresses; denim vests or jackets; gauzy cardigans or scarves; comfortable sandals; rain boots; washable canvas slip-ons or sneakers; lightweight cross-body bags; wire-rimmed sunglasses; sun hats

STEER CLEAR

white or light-colored bottoms; silk; any thick or heavy material meant for cooler months (ignore this for Glastonbury); cotton in colors that show perspiration (example: athletic gray t-shirts); miniskirts and dresses; denim skirts

RISKY BUSINESS

black (if this is your signature color, go for lightweight gauzy fabrics); embellished items (in small doses, preferably for a top or accessory); pants or jeans (go for a relaxed, lightweight pair that can easily be rolled up); short rompers (these can be a hassle in the bathroom)

CONCERT—PG. 36

New Year's EVE!

Break out the bubbly; it's time to talk about New Year's Eve! Touted as the most celebratory night of the year, NYE always comes with the unique pressure to have "the best night ever." While we can't promise that your plans will work out perfectly, we can advise you on how to create an ensemble that expresses just the right amount of sartorial merriment! *The goal is to create an outfit that's glamorous, dramatic, and nods to the theatricality of the evening.* Much like your Birthday Party look, traditional NYE attire should be striking—this is not the time for subtlety—and involve some shimmer in one way or another.

BEAUTY BOX

New Year's Eve is the perfect time to try a fun new hairstyle or makeup trend, whether that's a voluminous mane à la Brigitte Bardot or a deep wine lipstick that you saw on the fall runways. At the very least, make yourself feel extra special (like you would at your Birthday Party) and get a blowout or have your most cosmetically inclined friend do your makeup for the evening.

OTHER OUTFIT
IDEAS

1 metallic miniskirt +
semi-sheer tank +
cropped faux fur jacket

2 sexy LBD + sequined
jacket + metallic heels

3 body-con dress + silk
boyfriend blazer + lace
tights

GO FOR

metallics; jewel tones;
bright colors; eye-catching
fabrics, like lamé; black
dresses with dramatic
silhouettes; long-sleeve
mini dresses; sequined
shift dresses; black lace
miniskirts or tops; faux
fur vests or jackets;
capes or dressy trench
coats; glittery stilettos;
bold costume jewelry;
interesting hosiery
(opaque, swiss dot, sheer,
seamed, or lace)

STEER CLEAR

spring or summer colors
or fabrics; pale fabrics;
casual fabrics (cottons,
jerseys, knits); floral prints;
uncomfortable shoes or
dresses; jeans; leggings;
flats; delicate jewelry,
like stud earrings; overly
polished or natural hair
and makeup

RISKY BUSINESS

white (make sure it's a
heavy fabric, extra points
for white with sheen!);
jumpsuits or playsuits
in dressy fabrics (can
be annoying when you
go to the ladies' room);
button-downs (go for silky
materials or crisp, tuxedo
styles); pants; boots (go
for ankle booties instead
of thigh-high or knee-high
boots)

New Year's Eve is basically a rules-free night in terms of your wardrobe. Obviously you need to pick an ensemble that is dressy enough for the party you're attending, but generally you can rest assured that fancy cocktail attire is the norm. As is always true around the holidays, metallics are definitely an appropriate choice for this occasion, as are jewel tones, brights, and black. When picking your outfit, it's always nice to include at least one over-the-top element, whether that's via a sensational silhouette, an eye-popping color, or statement jewelry. Also, much like on your Girls' Night Out, you want to make sure your shoes are sexy and chic, but also easy-on-the-feet so you can walk and dance worry-free all night long. Last, but certainly not least, you need to think about how to stay warm in a stylish way. If you go for a mini dress, make it a long-sleeve mini dress. Prefer something that bares your shoulders? Don't forget to add a pair of opaque tights or a faux fur vest or coat.

When prepping for the big night, Hillary started with a strapless dress with a relatively straightforward, semi-short shape. The silhouette is pretty classic— the sweetheart neckline and slim skirt lend themselves to any color—but the gorgeous metallic fabric really elevates the frock and makes it spotlight-worthy. Since the gold dress is so shimmery, she passed on wearing lots of jewelry and went for an unexpected accessory instead: a tiny gold hat. The toy chapeau lends a touch of whimsy to her ensemble, which is just what NYE calls for. Finally, she picked a pair of black and metallic peep-toe platform pumps—perfect party shoes for this occasion!

As for Katherine's party-like-it's-1999 ensemble, she opted for a superchic maxi dress with an elegant asymmetrical design. Since her gown is solid black, she added a little texture with a faux fur vest—a glamorous, on-trend, and unusual outerwear choice. Of course, it wouldn't be New Year's Eve without a little sparkle, so she styled her dress with a pair of glittery black pumps and some collarbone-grazing earrings. The finishing touches came via a few bold beauty choices: a deep side part, strong '60s cat eyeliner, and a pop of bright red nail polish!

ON CAMERA

While not everyone dreams about being on camera—save for reality TV aspirants, budding actors, and broadcast journalism majors— knowing what to wear in such situations never hurts. *The goal is to create an uncomplicated and polished outfit that's more pulled together than a regular work ensemble, flatters your natural shape, and is appropriate for the demanding on-screen world.* After all, in these modern times, being media savvy and camera-ready/friendly is definitely considered a professional advantage. It makes sense, really: what boss wouldn't want someone who can step into the spotlight and represent the company stylishly? But no matter if the thought of getting mic'd makes you delighted or disturbed, one thing's for sure: there are lots of rules to consider when prepping an on-camera outfit. So many, in fact, we're just going to give you a list of our top dos and don'ts.

DON'TS FOR ON-CAMERA OUTFITS...

DON'T wear solid white or a color that strongly resembles white. It makes you look heavier and/or washed out.

DON'T wear anything baggy or billowy. The camera reads everything as two-dimensional, an effect that will add ten pounds.

DON'T wear tight/small patterns like checks, stripes, plaids, polka dots, and tiny floral prints. These types of patterns cause a moiré effect on camera, which means the patterns look like they're physically vibrating when seen through the lens.

DON'T wear jingly jewelry. Be wary of anything that might hit together and cause sound (this will be picked up by the microphone), as well as über-shiny jewelry that will pick up light and cause reflections.

*"Last, BUT NOT LEAST,
do keep in mind that you want your
audience to be focused on what you're
saying or doing—not on what
you're wearing—so KEEP IT SIMPLE."*

DOS FOR ON-CAMERA OUTFITS

DO choose bold colors—especially blues. They look great against your skin and will really make you pop onscreen.

DO find out what color your background will be before you get there. It's not always possible to have this information, but it's important because you don't want to wear something in a similar color.

DO bring a backup top or dress in a different color—just in case.

DO go for a dark neutral blazer (black, navy, or charcoal) over a colorful blouse or dress. It's flattering and slimming!

DO belt your dress or blouse, if possible, to accentuate your waist.

DO pick a slightly lower neckline or one that creates a "v." Anything that hits a few inches below your collarbone will almost always be more flattering than a higher neckline.

DO check that your outfit looks equally good when seated and standing.

DO make sure your clothes are perfectly pressed or steamed (this may mean getting dressed after you arrive at the filming location).

DO test your outfit. Just because something looks good in person, doesn't mean it will work on camera. If you can, try on your outfit and have a friend or family member take a quick photo of you, so you can see how the camera "reads" your look.

DO wear more makeup on camera than you would in real life. Bright lights can wash you out, so make sure you're wearing foundation, powder, blush (extremely important), eyeliner/shadow, and lipstick that is approximately a shade or two darker than your natural color. Give your makeup look the same camera test as your clothing.

OPERA

The GOAL is to create an outfit that embraces the opera's THEATRICAL side without falling victim to FUSSY wardrobe clichés.

True story: up until relatively recently, the closest we've come to opera exposure is watching the classic Looney Tunes cartoon "The Rabbit of Seville," featuring Bugs Bunny and Elmer Fudd. We know we're not the only philistines out there; for most people, going to the opera is not an everyday, or every decade, event, which is exactly why we're including it in this guidebook. Whether you're a Wagner buff or just want to recreate the scene in *Pretty Woman* when Richard Gere and Julia Roberts go to *La Traviata* (kudos if you wrangle a similarly impressive ruby necklace), the opera is an amazing opportunity to get dressed. The goal is to create an outfit that embraces the opera's theatrical side without falling victim to fussy wardrobe clichés. In other words: skip the long gloves, please.

When planning your opera ensemble, you should always check the dress code first—La Scala in Milan is dressier than the Metropolitan Opera in New York, for example—especially when it's opening night. Those special performances call for fancier attire, but for most in-season shows you can wear anything ranging from casual nighttime ensembles (see Art Gallery) to polished party attire (see Corporate Cocktail Party). If you are going to the season's first show or the premiere of a new production, pay homage to opera's grand history and take the more formal route, which means a dress that would be appropriate for an evening

wedding or a black-tie event.

We decided to show you options for what we'd wear to an opening night at the opera, as it's a bit more fun to take the dramatic route! Katherine picked an incredible white tulle dress with graphic black beading and a neon green corset underlay. The one-shoulder ruffled neckline is incredible, so to show it off she slicked her hair back into a full bun and added a pair of oversized stud earrings. To keep things youthful, she skipped hosiery and opted for a pair of glittery pumps with a moderate heel, which will be perfect for the opera house's stairs. Finally she added a tiny, shiny shoulder bag that's just big enough for a lipstick and her opera glasses!

Hillary wanted to wear something super-striking without going the typical ball gown route, so she opted for a floor-length black dress with long sleeves as the foundation of her opera ensemble. To add interest to the simple silhouette, she added a studded leather belt at her natural waist and then threw on an oversized faux fur bolero. The jacket is definitely dramatic, but the all-black palette keeps it chic and saves it from looking campy. The monochromatic ensemble also allows her to have fun with the accessories, so she finished the look with a few equally bold pieces, including a statement necklace, multiple chunky bangles, and a metallic sequin clutch. The result is perfect for a night of drama!

OTHER OUTFIT IDEAS

1 tuxedo suit + silky shell/bustier + red lipstick

2 bold-colored one-shoulder dress + black strappy heels + slicked back hair

3 metallic cocktail dress + sheer black tights + black pumps

GO FOR

fun cocktail dresses with interesting details (like a one-shoulder silhouette, full skirt, or sheer sleeves); floor-length gowns; faux fur vests or boleros; trophy jackets or embellished boleros; fancy wraps; sparkly statement shoes; tiny evening clutches; rhinestone jewelry; polished updos

STEER CLEAR

jeans (opening night or not, have some respect for the arts!); miniskirts or dresses; sundresses; sweaters (go for an oversized scarf, shawl, trophy jacket, or bolero instead); shorts; flats; hats

RISKY BUSINESS

easily wrinkled fabrics, like silk or lightweight satin; blazers (make sure it's a fitted tuxedo-style jacket worn over a formal dress); super-slim skirts (just make sure you can sit easily)

PICNIC

While we certainly do love a perfectly appointed table, dressed with loads of lovely linens and fabulous flatware, there's something so fun about dining alfresco. Whether you're on a bench in the middle of a park or sitting in an amphitheater listening to music, picnics are one of our favorite adventures to plan. In addition to picking and packing the perfect edibles—charcuterie, spiced marcona almonds, and rosé for us!—choosing the ideal outfit is always fun too. Much like the menu, when it comes to the appropriate clothing choices for a picnic, you're free to experiment with a wide range of options. *The goal is to create a casually cute outfit that is relatively indestructible and conducive to sitting on the ground.* But don't think that just because you're wearing heartier duds means you can go sloppy: you still can, and should, look sharp!

When planning your picnic outfit, remember: patterns are your friends. Whether it's a cheerful check or a bold graphic, it's always a good idea to go for a print playsuit or pair of shorts. In addition to their inherently festive quality, prints are a very practical choice, as they will camouflage any potential stains (grass, dirt, food drippings) far better than a solid-colored fabric could. Also, make sure your potential ensemble passes the "sit test," which is exactly what it sounds like. Make sure that everything is comfortable and covered, and that nothing is pulling or gaping in an unattractive way. On that note, generally speaking, wearing something with a full silhouette—

whether that's a wide-leg pair of shorts or a circle skirt—is never a bad idea. Also remember that you'll be on the grass, so choose shoes that won't sink into the ground: no stilettos!

For her prospective picnic outfit, Katherine opted for a darling gingham skirt with a full silhouette as the foundation of her look. This piece works for a number of reasons: the generous cut means she can sit comfortably on the grass, the print references traditional picnic textiles in a cheeky way, and the skirt's subtle slate gray color is fresh, unexpected, and keeps the kitchyness to a minimum. Her lightweight gray cashmere t-shirt is sheer enough to work on a warm day, but cozy enough to forgo bringing outerwear. Since this is a playful, informal occasion, she added a simple pair of sneakers and an armful of colorful bracelets and bangles, and then finished things off with a vintage-inspired pair of sunglasses.

Hillary also picked shorts for her picnic ensemble, albeit via a cute romper. The playsuit has generously full legs, which gives it a more feminine vibe and ensures she can sit on the ground with ease. The long caramel cardigan is a nice addition, because it gives the look a little more interest, breaks up the bright print, and ensures she'll be equipped for a change in temperatures. As for Hillary's accessories, she picked a few summer-friendly pieces, including a wide-brimmed straw hat (chic sun protection), woven tote, and denim wedges.

OTHER OUTFIT IDEAS

1 knee-length jean shorts + lightweight boyfriend shirt with cuffed sleeves + huaraches

2 lightweight print maxi dress + woven/canvas belt + jean jacket + soft scarf

3 overalls + tank top + low-top canvas sneakers

GO FOR

machine-washable fabrics; lightweight knits; gingham and liberty prints; wide-leg shorts and playsuits; full skirts; lightweight cardigans and sweaters; semi-sheer sweaters; simple sneakers; flat sandals; ballet flats; oxfords; moccasins; bright or woven totes; sun hats; oversized lightweight scarves

STEER CLEAR

delicate or dry-clean–only fabrics; white; silk; anything with intricate straps; workwear; body-con minis or dresses; low-rise shorts or pants; bikini tops (save this for the Beach & Pool); stilettos

RISKY BUSINESS

maxi dresses or skirts (make sure the fabric isn't too heavy); jean shorts (do they pass the "sit test" or not?); pants (nothing too tight or low-rise; short skirts

POLO & HORSE RACES

The GOAL is to create an outfit that is feminine and festive, yet simple enough that it doesn't compete with your HAT.

Before you head out to the polo grounds, go to a major racing event like the Kentucky Derby, or round up your friends for an afternoon of betting on the ponies, remember that equestrian events call for a certain amount of sartorial flair. There are also some hard-and-fast wardrobe rules, so be sure to check the destination's requirements for specific yeas or nays. (For example, at the week-long Royal Ascot in England, it's mandatory for all women attending the races to wear a hat, and only formal day dresses are allowed!) Generally speaking, the goal is to create an outfit that is feminine and festive, yet simple enough that it doesn't compete with your hat. Also keep in mind that most polo matches fall on the casual side of the spectrum, unless it's a charity event or a big event/ tournament.

When considering your outfit, it's always a good idea to opt for light or bright colors, as you will most likely be outside and in the sun for the majority of the day. Dresses are the gold standard; just make sure that the silhouette is in line with the

dress code. As for your footwear, go for comfortable heels and remember to wear wedges if you're going to be on the grass at all. (Especially if you're going to be stomping divots!)

For a day at the races, Katherine picked a pale blue pinstripe dress with short sleeves as the anchor of her look. The stripe is a subtle nod to summer seersucker and has a hint of preppiness that's perfect for this occasion. She cinched in the waist of her dress with a raffia belt and added a light pink linen blazer, then finished her outfit with her favorite tortoiseshell sunglasses and brown heels.

Hillary created a more traditional ensemble for her day at the races, starting with a turquoise fifties-style dress with a full skirt. While a hat can be a hardworking accessory, she picked one that's more aesthetically pleasing than functional. The jaunty pink straw chapeau definitely makes a sweet statement, so she kept the rest of her look neutral with a pair of nude platform pumps and a simple clutch

OTHER OUTFIT
IDEAS

1 pleated circle skirt + dressy sleeveless blouse + standout pumps

2 paperbag dress shorts + feminine blouse + lightweight blazer + wood platforms

3 full-skirt sundress + gold flats + cream cardigan + raffia clutch

GO FOR

light or bright colors for day; prints (polka dots, stripes, seersucker); sundresses with full skirts; trench coats; linen suits; wedges or espadrilles; comfortable pumps with more substantial heels; hats; lightweight wraps or shawls; sunglasses; sunscreen

STEER CLEAR

heavy dark fabrics; denim; leather; anything too short, too tight, or too revealing; shorts; turtlenecks; pants; t-shirts; stilettos

RISKY BUSINESS

maxi dresses (make sure that your shoes are high enough to avoid dragging); strapless dresses; shorts (some events require women to wear skirts or dresses)

RAIN

The GOAL is to create a functional outfit that uses different TEXTURES, layers, and colors to show some flair.

Soggy days are the worst: you want to stay dry of course, but most weather-repellent essentials are so utilitarian they actually look u-g-l-y. But just because the forecast calls for drizzle doesn't mean you always have to sacrifice your personal style—you simply need to get creative! The goal is to create a functional outfit that uses different textures, layers, and colors to show some flair.

It's okay to think outside the box: just because something isn't specifically made for precipitation doesn't mean it can't work well in it! You should also try to make your outfit as nuanced as possible. Since this isn't a great time to experiment with silhouette, instead pick unexpected colors and textures to add interest. By wearing a combination of materials—shiny patent, nubby knits, and basic matte items—you'll look more stylish, even if you're all covered up or insist on a monochromatic palette. Stay away from wide-leg pants and maxi skirts when it's gross outside, as both styles will no doubt drag in the rain and soak up the puddles, making you miserable, cold, and wet. Stick to skinny silhouettes, cropped hemlines, and skirt-and-tights combos instead.

Whenever the forecast calls for inclement weather, Hillary breaks out her go-to galoshes, so she built her outfit around these boots. Instead of reaching for skinny jeans—which also work well with rain boots—she opted for a thick pair of tights and a denim shirtdress. Though a dress isn't always an obvious rainy-day pick, it can be a smart choice if you go with a sturdy fabric or a relaxed silhouette. Rather than grabbing a basic black slicker, Hillary picked a wine-colored patent raincoat; the dark hue is still practical, but the rich tone is a decidedly interesting choice. Finally she added a lightweight scarf in a cheerful melon hue to perk up the whole outfit and inject some energy into the gray day.

While Katherine opted for neutral colors for her rainy-day ensemble, she kept things interesting through her choice of knits. She started with a thin, long-sleeve t-shirt and a thick gray cable-knit sweater, and then added a chunky woven scarf in a muted mauve color for contrast. Since those two pieces are bulky, she selected a formfitting pair of jeans (notice how they're skinny enough to slip into boots?), a windowpane wool blazer to add some polish to the outfit, and covered everything with a water-resistant anorak. That last layer will protect her from the elements, but, thanks to the drawstring waist, still shows a bit of shape. As for her footwear, Katherine went for a pair of platform ankle boots, a favorite option also discussed in Cold Weather. The platform boots keep your foot up and away from the cold puddles, ensuring your feet will stay dry and feel warm!

OTHER OUTFIT
IDEAS

1 carrot trousers + long-sleeve t-shirt + trench coat + ankle boots

2 skinny jeans + rain boots + long, striped t-shirt + anorak

3 wool mini dress + lace-up booties + opaque tights + trench coat

GO FOR

layers; sweaters; hooded jackets and coats; skinny jeans; cropped pants; skirts or dresses and tights; trench coats; water-resistant anoraks; chunky knit sweaters and scarves; platform booties; rubber rain boots; brimmed hats; bucket hats; colorful scarves; chic umbrellas

STEER CLEAR

white; silk or other water-spot-friendly fabrics; faux (or real) fur; leather and suede; wide-leg jeans or pants; maxi skirts; voluminous skirts or dresses; felt or knit hats; flat irons (embrace your natural waves on rainy days)

RISKY BUSINESS

wool or cashmere (they'll keep you warm but natural fibers can smell in the rain, so make sure you wear these fabrics under a water-resistant layer); skirts and dresses (add a pair of warm tights and boots); heels (go for a platform or wedge); platform pumps

RELIGIOUS OCCASION: *DAY*

The GOAL is to create an outfit that is respectful of the occasion; translation: modest and conservative.

Let's say you're invited to some sort of daytime religious occasion—like a baptism, Easter Sunday service, or a bar/bat mitzvah—which makes you anxious because you're either nonpracticing or nonreligious, and simply non-certain about attire at said event. No worries! The good thing about these social situations is that they typically take place in a house of worship, which means there are specific dress codes to follow. Even if the event doesn't occur in a church or synagogue, the ceremony will be lead by a representative of one of those places, so the wardrobe guidelines still apply. The goal is to create an outfit that is respectful of the occasion; translation: modest and conservative.

While the exact dress code rules vary, it's always a good idea to err on the traditional side for daytime religious occasions. That means making sure your shoulders are covered—no strapless dresses, unless paired with a jacket or cardigan—and that your hemline is at least knee-length or longer. Also, though this should probably go without saying, this is not the appropriate time for body-conscious clothing or anything ultra-tight. Instead, pick something feminine and tailored, in the vein of what you'd wear to a Graduation or La-dies' Luncheon, but following the aforementioned rules. Also, while you're certainly permitted to wear black, it's always nice to opt for lighter neutrals and a more festive palette if possible.

The wardrobe buzzword for these events is "ladylike," so Katherine chose a gray silk tank with a simple print and collarbone-grazing neckline, which she tucked into an olive green linen skirt. Since her top is sleeveless, she added an ivory cardigan with three-quarter sleeves to make it more appropriate for the occasion. As far as accessories go, she wore her usual daytime bag and an appropriately classic pair of gray pumps, and kept her jewelry and makeup on the minimal side.

Hillary also went for a vintage-inspired propriety for her daytime religious occasion look and picked a simple short-sleeve shift dress. While the dress's slim silhouette would be perfectly on-point in another fabric or color, the combination of the lace overlay and the blush color make it a little more special and memorable. To complete her look, Hillary accessorized with three timeless pieces—a structured bag, nude pumps, and a pale khaki trench—the addition of which result in a truly polished ensemble.

OTHER OUTFIT IDEAS

1 floral maxi dress + gauzy cardigan + woven wedges

2 jewel-tone dress with ¾-length sleeves + black patent belt + black patent heels

3 long-sleeve print blouse + tweed pencil skirt + point-toe pumps

GO FOR

simple prints, like pinstripes, polka dots, or soft florals; maxi skirts or dresses; pencil skirts; silk blouses; fine-knit cardigans; ladylike dresses; trench coats; modest heels; structured day bags; natural makeup

STEER CLEAR

loud graphic prints and oversized/excessive logos; lingerie details or body-conscious styles; anything low-cut, short, strapless, or sleeveless; denim; leather; studs or rhinestones; sneakers, flip-flops; nightclub pumps; noisy or jingly bracelets or necklaces

RISKY BUSINESS

sheer fabrics; pants (if dress code allows, go for a formal fabric like a wool or silk blend and pair with a feminine top and complementary jacket); tights (skip anything patterned or lacy)

RELIGIOUS OCCASION: *NIGHT*

In the grand scheme of things, there aren't too many religious occasions that take place at night. But you never know when you'll get called on the bar/bat mitzvah circuit, so it's always a good idea to be prepared. Most of the wardrobe ideas behind your nighttime look should be similar to the thoughts you use to construct your daytime religious occasion ensemble. *The goal is to create a cocktail outfit that embraces the house of worship's dress code, but with slightly more festive accessories that are appropriate for evening.*

A good rule of thumb is to pick something that's a little bit more conservative than what you'd wear to a cocktail party or wedding, unless the invitation or your host specifies something fancier. As always, keeping your shoulders covered is a must, and we definitely suggest sticking to modest silhouettes and hemlines. One way to make sure your ensemble is sundown chic is to include an item with some sheen or shimmer. That can mean a silky dress, satin trench, or an embellished jacket—the possibilities are endless. Additionally, while we recommend sticking to small or subtle jewelry for daytime religious occasions, you can break out some slightly bolder baubles. Of course your footwear is another way to inject some personality in your outfit, so a pretty pump in a unique color or a classic heel with an unexpected accent (like a big bow on the toe, for example) would definitely work here.

With propriety in mind, Katherine started her outfit with a black pencil skirt that hit just below her knee. The hemline is longer than what she'd normally wear to a cocktail party, but it's perfect for this occasion. She paired the skirt with a long-sleeve lace blouse worn over a nude camisole and then added a satin trench. This combination works because the lace top shows her personal style, while the lightweight coat makes the ensemble a little more modest for the ceremony portion of the evening. Finishing touches came via a chunky necklace (dressing up her look even more, showing her individuality), green snake print peep-toe pumps (injecting color into the outfit), and a zipper-detail navy-blue clutch (a cool, unexpected choice).

As for Hillary's nighttime religious occasion look, she picked a classic black chiffon dress as the foundation of her ensemble. It's a totally timeless silhouette and material, plus it has a moderate neckline that befits the occasion. The beaded bolero with long sleeves elevates her outfit and makes it more appropriate. Since the hemline of her dress is a smidge on the high side for a religious occasion, she added sheer black tights and opted for unfussy black pumps with a moderate heel. Finally, to complete her outfit, she added a metallic clutch and a multichain gold necklace, both of which are subtle enough to work with the metallic trophy jacket without overpowering it.

OTHER OUTFIT IDEAS

1. long-sleeve dark neutral cocktail dress + sheer black tights + black embellished pumps

2. dark-colored dressy pencil skirt + metallic top + cropped wool coat

3. cap-sleeve black lace dress + patent pumps + cape coat

GO FOR

dark colors like black, navy, or charcoal gray; LBDs (in this case we mean LONG black dress); long-sleeve cocktail dresses; long skirts or dresses; pencil skirts; silk blouses; sharp blazers; oversized clutches or evening bags; embellished outerwear; cocktail rings or bib necklaces; opaque tights

STEER CLEAR

anything low-cut or short; anything strapless or sleeveless without an appropriate jacket; denim; leather; animal prints; loud graphic prints; logos; studs; sandals; noisy or jingly bracelets or necklaces

RISKY BUSINESS

sheer fabrics; pants (if dress code allows, pair with a feminine top and complementary jacket); trench coats (choose a dark color in a finer fabric, like silk or satin); tights

REUNION: FAMILY

Families are funny: on one hand, they can be your greatest source of comfort, but they can also stress you out to the extreme. But no matter if they're terrific or terrible, close or distant, big or small, at some point they will gather, and you will be expected to attend. Now, these events inherently involve a great number of variables and everything depends on the family itself and the location, so giving advice for this sort of social situation is a bit of a tricky game. *The goal is to create an outfit that is appropriate for both the specific location and your family.* After all, clearly what you wear to a huge multigenerational barbecue on your uncle's farm in Oklahoma should be different than what you'd pick for a formal dinner party to celebrate your grandmother's eightieth birthday at a four-star restaurant in San Francisco. As such, please feel free to refer to similar occasions in this book for guidance.

When assembling an outfit for a family event, there are a few general guidelines to keep in mind. Generally speaking, these situations mean you'll come into contact with some people you're very close with and others you haven't seen in a long time, so it's always a good idea to be comfortable and look polished. Also, since it is a family occasion, there will probably be a wide range of ages in attendance, so we suggest going for a more modest look. If you feel as though it's necessary to show off an edgy look—which is a little questionable, but fine—just make sure that you're not showing too much skin. Of course, our argument against that is the fact that these events invari-

ably involve a ton of photographs, so why not wear something a little more timeless that won't embarrass you years down the road. In other words: save the hot trends for your next Girls' Night Out!

Much like for a School Reunion, your family event outfit should be something you feel secure and confident wearing, so Katherine picked her favorite long-sleeve LBD as the base of her look and then added a tribal-print wrap cardi-coat. The print shows off her taste (as does the fact that she belted it), but the neutral color palette makes it a little more classic. She paired this ensemble with of-the-moment lace-up ankle boots and balanced their trendiness by selecting a ladylike frame bag in charcoal gray.

Hillary also picked a dress for this occasion, though she selected a ruffled wrap dress with a tiny print. Since her dress is on the shorter side, she turned to a time-honored trick for making a brief hemline look more modest: opaque black tights. The tights, coupled with a simple pair of black ankle booties, give the whole ensemble more coverage, which is perfect for more conservative families or occasions. While we hesitate to recommend jeans for most family events—ultracasual situations excluded, of course—you can work some denim in via a jacket, as Hillary did. Though the shrunken jacket is less formal, her dress and the sophisticated, structured purse balance it perfectly. Finally, since her outfit is primarily composed of neutrals, she added a bold red scarf as a nod to her personality.

OTHER OUTFIT
IDEAS

1 cuffed khakis + striped top + ballet flats

2 feminine dress + denim jacket + wooden wedges

3 black long-sleeve mini + print tights + flats

GO FOR

timeless silhouettes; girly dresses; your favorite LBD; shrunken denim jackets; wrap sweaters or dresses; trench coats; polished blazers; ankle boots; ballet flats; fun tights (prints, patterns); interesting accessories; colorful scarves

STEER CLEAR

anything too edgy; clothing or accessories that are too trendy and will look dated in photos; lingerie details; matching t-shirts (they may be spirited, but they're never chic!); short shorts or miniskirts; sweatshirts and sweatpants; overly trendy hair and makeup (you want to look like yourself)

RISKY BUSINESS

leather (too much leather looks harsh, so keep it minimal, like a cropped leather jacket or vest and balance with a feminine dress); jeans (save jeans for the most casual of families/reunions and pair them with something nicer than a t-shirt—also stay away from too much distressing)

REUNION: SCHOOL

We love a challenge and have more than a touch of competitive spirit, which is why we adore discussing what to wear to a school reunion. It's such a strange and nerve-wracking occasion—who really wants to revisit their teenage years anyway?—which is part of what also makes it so exciting. While some people freak themselves out, musing about how they've changed (or how they haven't), we say: don't worry about who you were, just focus on who you are now and embrace it. You owe that to your younger self!

The goal is to create an outfit that makes you feel comfortable and confident, without looking like you're trying too hard. Clearly you want to look fashionable, but you also want to look professional and polished, too. Ideally,

your ensemble should communicate who you truly are today— the best version, of course!

Though it might sound counterintuitive, we don't recommend getting a new outfit for your high school or college reunion. There are too many things that can go wrong, and it's kind of a waste of your time, energy, and money. Instead, our suggestion is to wear something you already own and love. Do you have a dress that always makes you feel fabulous? Is there an outfit you gravitate toward when you want to feel sleek and chic? These are excellent starting points for your reunion look.

Shoot for an ensemble that is a mixture of what you'd wear to a Corporate Cocktail Party and on a First Date: flirty, but sophisticated. Whatever you

> **" The goal is to create an outfit that makes you feel comfortable and confident, without looking like you're trying too hard. "**

"Instead of buying a new outfit, wear something you already own and love."

GO FOR

classic silhouettes; solid colors; party dresses; fitted jackets; pencil skirts; feminine blouses; little leather jackets; crisp blazers; statement shoes; interesting clutches; personality-showing jewelry; polished hair and makeup

STEER CLEAR

sequins; bright bold prints; jeans; red lipstick; bold/trendy makeup

RISKY BUSINESS

animal prints (these are great, but wear them in small doses as accents like Katherine did); body-conscious dresses (wear with a modest neckline and hemline or accessorize with blazer); updos (make sure there's a casual element to your outfit—you don't want to look "prom"—and go for a style you could have done yourself); bold makeup (if you go for a red lip, keep the rest of your look simple and make sure you have your lipstick on standby for touch-ups)

OTHER OUTFIT IDEAS

1. solid-color jumpsuit + statement belt + open-toe pumps

2. floral dress + fitted leather jacket + gray suede heels

3. leather skirt + crisp white button-up blouse + snake print peep-toe pumps

4. fitted tweed dress + waist belt + platform pumps + patent clutch

5. dark neutral bandage skirt + slouchy tank + boxy blazer + nude heels

STYLE SUGGESTION

Do not, under any circumstances, wear your sexiest outfit, something really trendy, or get crazy with your hair and makeup. You will look tragic and desperate—we promise. Show off ONE of your best assets. Waist: wear a great belt. Arms: sleeveless or strapless dress or top. Legs: shorter skirt or dress.

"Shoot for an ensemble that's a mix of what you'd wear to a Corporate Cocktail Party and on a First Date: flirty, but sophisticated."

wear, we do recommend spending a little money on two important things: a great blowout and a killer pair of shoes. Both are instant mood-boosters and foolproof ways to feel fabulous.

While high school/college reunions can vary based on the location, Hillary always goes for a little black dress. In this case, she picked a simple knee length version with white stitching at the waist, hem, and straps. It's formfitting without being skintight, and the dress's clean, classic lines are appropriate and elegant for this occasion. To add a little toughness to her look, she opted for a neutral clutch with stud details, then finished the outfit with two silver cuffs.

Katherine feels most confident in a short dress, so she picked an abbreviated white dress with a ruffled skirt for this event. To make the frock a little less flirty and a little more professional, she added a sharp black jacket and pulled her hair back into a neat chignon. Since Katherine adores accessories, she included several statement pieces in her outfit—including bold gold earrings, a gold cuff, an animal-print clutch, and snake print peep-toe pumps—to show off her style and personalize her outfit.

*R*oad TRIP

If there is anything more fun than taking a road trip with your best friends, we haven't done it yet and frankly doubt that it exists. Seriously, what could be better than experiencing miles of open road with your nearest and dearest, especially when that means you get to enjoy their company, your favorite songs, and tons of ridiculous snacks? In fact, it might be the one time in life we agree with that old saying, "the journey is the destination." *The goal is to create an outfit that is conducive to long hours of sitting without being too sloppy for public viewing.*

Basically you want something with the ease of sweats but more stylish, something similar to the looks you might wear for Errands or Weekends. Remember, the journey always involves pit stops, snack breaks, and sightseeing, so you need to look presentable for these out-of-car moments.

In addition to comfort, we've found that lightweight layers are often of paramount importance. Obviously if you're tooling around Maui or barreling through Minnesota in the middle of winter, being prepared for changing temperatures is probably not a primary concern, but it's a good idea to keep your options open when in less extreme climates. Though this probably goes without saying, your fabric choice is important here, too: wrinkle-resistant, lightweight, casual materials are the best. Also, even if you're not stain-prone, it's always wise to stay away from light colors. Patterns are a great option, as

they will mask any spills or stains you might get along the way.

Katherine's top road-trip pick is a pair of slouchy denim shorts; they're super-baggy, so she can sit for hours without getting annoyed by a tight waistband. She added a thin, boxy blouse with a slightly wrinkled textured for her top and made sure to bring an oversized fabric hobo, too. The long-strap bag is key because it's big enough to house some lightweight layers, like a cardigan and a scarf. Extra layers are important for a number of reasons, like the fact that your copilot's idea of a comfortable temperature might feel ice-cold to you. Also, a soft sweater or jacket can double as a nice pillow, should you decided to take a disco nap. Necessary accessories: a big pair of shades to shield you from the glare and some easy sandals.

Another great idea for a road trip is a maxi skirt, which is what Hillary picked. She opted for a vibrant orange skirt in a sturdy cotton, an airy-yet-cozy selection. With her unencumbered lower half set, she added a few easy layers on top, including a neutral taupe t-shirt, her favorite denim button-up, and a beloved green parka. As discussed for rain outfits, an anorak with a drawstring waist is always a flattering choice, as it gives you a hint of shape without being aggressively body conscious. Hillary opted for easy accessories too: beaded flat sandals, a simple brown snake print sack, and a pair of retro sunglasses.

OTHER OUTFIT
IDEAS

1 slouchy, cuffed khakis + tank top + chambray shirt + moccasins

2 leggings + oversized button-up + ballet flats

3 comfortable pair of jeans + boho peasant top + huaraches

GO FOR

fabrics that have a crinkly texture or that won't wrinkle; lightweight, soft layers; loose shorts or pants; full skirts; gauzy button-ups; loose maxi dresses; slip-on shoes; across-body bags; oversized scarves (can double as a pillow or blanket); oversized shades; natural makeup

STEER CLEAR

linen or silk; tight, uncomfortable jeans; miniskirts; short shorts; body-con skirts or dresses; lace-up boots or strappy sandals with multiple buckles; tall boots that are hard to get on and off in the confines of your seat

RISKY BUSINESS

light colors (if you want to wear a stain-showing shade, make sure it involves a pattern, which will help conceal any food/drink drips); jeans (go for a pair with some stretch or a slouchy cut)

Shopping

The GOAL is to create an EASY-to-remove outfit that allows YOU to change efficiently.

No matter if you're a bona fide boutique addict who spends all her free time browsing her favorite stores or someone who rarely gets to dedicate a day to hitting the non-virtual racks (that's us!), everyone must shop sometimes. When the need for new clothing calls, it's always a good idea to answer that request wearing an ensemble that's conducive to the task at hand.

The goal is to create an easy-to-remove outfit that allows you to change efficiently. All practicalities aside, this is also a fun time to try some of the more fashion-forward casual items in your wardrobe or to experiment with a trend or look that's recently caught your eye—just make sure to consider these key aspects before you go!

> " Before you hit the mall or your favorite store, think about what you're shopping for and pick an outfit that will aid that plan. "

1. Forget about extreme shoes.

Though you are spending the day in pursuit of all the best fashion out there, that doesn't mean this is the ideal time to break out your most of-the-moment shoes. Ideally, your shoes will be a) walking friendly and b) easily slipped on and off, so if a killer pair of pumps catches your interest, you can quickly try them on. That said, if you are shopping for pants or something where the length of the hemline is a major concern or focus, it's a good idea to bring your shoes shopping with you. Of course, if they satisfy the above conditions set forth in a) and b), go ahead and wear them!

STYLE SUGGESTION

If you're shopping some-where that doesn't have a dressing room (like a flea market or some vintage stores), make sure you have a thought-out "base" outfit before you go. A thin slip dress is always a good option: you can easily slip on pants under the dress, or try on prospective purchases over it without compromising the fit.

OTHER OUTFIT IDEAS

1. slouchy, cuffed jeans + slim tank + cropped trench + loafers

2. dark maxi skirt + slip-on sandals + draped t-shirt + across-body bag

3. cigarette jeans + lightweight gray pullover + leather jacket + flat ankle boots

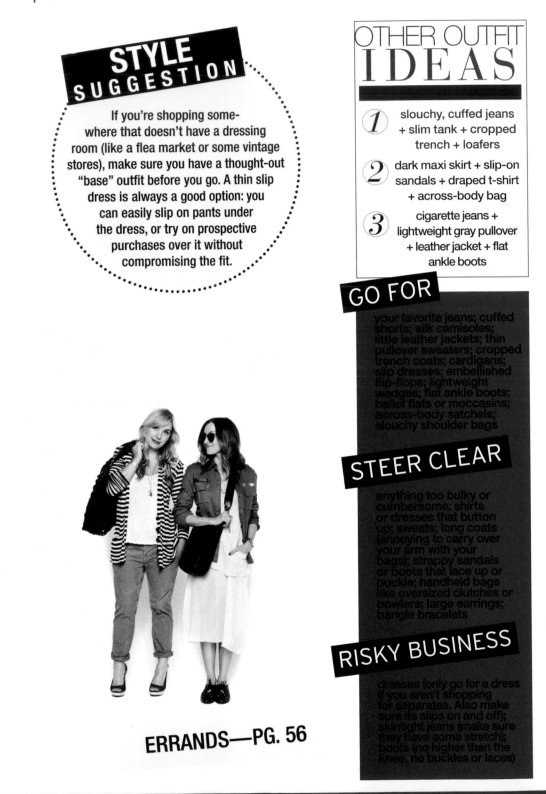

GO FOR

your favorite jeans; cuffed shorts; silk camisoles; little leather jackets; thin pullover sweaters; cropped trench coats; cardigans; slip dresses; embellished flip-flops; lightweight wedges; flat ankle boots; ballet flats or moccasins; across-body satchels; slouchy shoulder bags

STEER CLEAR

anything too bulky or cumbersome; shirts or dresses that button up; sweats; long coats (annoying to carry over your arm with your bags); strappy sandals or boots that lace up or buckle; handheld bags like oversized clutches or bowlers; large earrings; bangle bracelets

RISKY BUSINESS

dresses (only go for a dress if you aren't shopping for separates. Also make sure its slips on and off); skintight jeans (make sure they have some stretch); boots (no higher than the knee, no buckles or laces)

ERRANDS—PG. 56

"*Though you are spending the day in pursuit of all the best fashion out there, that doesn't mean this is the ideal time to break out your most of-the-moment shoes.*"

2. Let your shopping goals guide your outfit.

Before you hit the mall or your favorite store, think about what you're shopping for and pick an outfit that will aid that plan. For example, if you're planning on looking for tops or jeans, make sure you're wearing separates before you leave the house. A dress will complicate matters; unless you take entire outfits into the dressing room, you'll end up topless or bottomless. Either way that means you can't leave the room to show your friends a specific piece or check out your potential purchase in a different mirror, which is annoying.

Conversely, if buying a new dress is on the top of your to-do list, your shopping outfit should consist of an uncomplicated frock—like a cotton slip dress—that you can take off and put on quickly. (Bonus points for picking a dress in a sturdy fabric that won't wrinkle when it's thrown on the dressing room floor.)

3. Wear one of your wardrobe essentials.

We've all had that moment in the dressing room, pondering whether this sweater will look cute with our favorite black pants or if this skirt has the right proportions to wear with our go-to little leather jacket. Instead of wondering or trying to visualize how this new item will work with the essentials you already own, try to include at least one in your shopping outfit. It just makes things easier!

With these maxims in mind, Katherine created her shopping outfit around two different cotton slip dresses: a short nude style and a longer black iteration. The short nude dress is a perfect foundation piece and will answer the question "Does this dress need a slip?" before she can even ask it, while the longer black layer gives a little coverage and texture to her ensemble. With her base set, she added her favorite cropped khaki jacket (a weekend staple), a long pendant (easy to remove and an important detail to try with prospective purchases to give them a little personality), and a chic pair of shades.

As for her shoes, she went for complete comfort in a pair of chain-detailed flip-flops that she can easily remove throughout the day. Bag-wise, she picked a large across-body bag that keeps her hands free for flipping through the racks.

Hillary, on the other hand, opted for her favorite pair of bell-bottom jeans. To keep things comfortable, she picked a slightly oversized, lightweight, graphic t-shirt and then added a cropped blazer to give the overall look a little polish. To make shopping even easier, she opted for a pair of gray ankle booties that slip off and an oversized satchel. The purse has both long and shorter straps, so she can wear it as a tote or on her shoulder, depending on how many shopping bags she's holding!

SIGHTSEEING

The GOAL is to create an outfit that's comfortable, CASUAL, and composed of neutral wardrobe BASICS.

It's challenging enough figuring out what to wear when you're home and have full access to your closet, let alone when you're traveling and have limited resources, which is probably why we get so many questions about what to wear when sightseeing. Whether you're off to take in the natural splendor of the Grand Canyon or have a gondola ride down the Grand Canal planned, don't think that just because you need to wear something functional and practical means you can't look cute. The goal is to create an outfit that's comfortable, casual, and composed of neutral wardrobe basics. It might be something similar to what you'd wear on the Weekends or for running Errands, but with an even greater emphasis on foot-friendly shoes.

Since most itineraries are jam-packed and require you to be out and about exploring the scene, obviously you want to create an ensemble that's easy to wear for long periods of time. Now, that doesn't mean you can get away with wearing the "rude American" uniform of sweats or leggings and a baggy t-shirt—oh the visual horror! Instead, look chic by packing your favorite essentials—things like stretchy skinny jeans, cuffed trousers, cute cardigans, and simple tops—in a primarily neutral palette. By sticking to that palette (black, white, gray, navy, khaki, army green, tan), you ensure a few things: a) most pieces will work together, so you can combine things multiple ways and get more wear out of each item; b) with the exception of white, these colors don't look dirty immediately; and c) you won't stand out to the locals as an obvious tourist. Of course,

if a bag filled with all neutrals sounds super-boring to you, just throw in a handful of bright accents, like a vibrant semi-sheer scarf if it's summer or a bold beret in the colder months. It's also important to pick your fabrics carefully; skip anything that's easily wrinkled or dry-clean only and go for sturdy, lightweight materials that allow for easy layering.

For example, Hillary wanted to create a look that would work for a cool-weather trip, so she started with one of her go-to pieces: a stretchy pair of black skinny jeans. She added a long-sleeve striped top—a universally appealing choice—and a heavy cotton anorak for a little warmth and to give her outfit a touch of structure. She picked a pair of classic lace-up sneakers for her footwear and added a long-strap suede bag (can be worn on the shoulder or across the body) and a thin, striped scarf, which gives her whole look a jaunty air.

Katherine, on the other hand, decided to mix lots of tiny prints together to create her sightseeing look. She opted for a relaxed pair of conductor-stripe shorts, which work because they're generously cut, super-soft, and slightly dressier than denim cutoffs. She then added a flowy gingham top, so she can enjoy the local food without feeling constricted, and a floppy liberty-print fabric hat. To carry a day's worth of belongings (binoculars, cardigan, maps, water bottle, and sunblock), she picked a lightweight across-body bag in a washable canvas. Finally, she selected a perfectly broken-in pair of sandals with no stiff straps or thongs, which guarantees her feet will stay blister-free all day.

OTHER OUTFIT IDEAS

1 knee-length peasant skirt + lightweight t-shirt + moccasins

2 skinny jeans + long-sleeve t-shirt + trench coat + canvas slip-ons

3 capri jeans + gray tank + tan cardigan + low-top tennis shoes + red scarf

GO FOR

neutral-colored layers; cardigans; soft t-shirts and tanks; cargo pants or shorts; cropped jeans; cuffed denim shorts; broken-in sandals; low-top tennis shoes; moccasins; flat boots (for the winter); fabric or canvas totes or across-body bags; lightweight print scarves; fabric or canvas hats that will easily fold

STEER CLEAR

silk or linen fabrics; anything that's dry-clean only; a suitcase full of colorful clothing; crisp button-ups; overly distressed jeans or shorts; tight pants or jeans with no stretch; oversized t-shirts; sweats; bathing suits; heels; brand-new shoes; designer bags

RISKY BUSINESS

prints (either use in small accents like a scarf or make sure all of your prints live harmoniously together—otherwise it's a waste to pack something you can only wear once)

Somber
OCCASION

Sadly, somber occasions are one of life's inevitabilities. Though no one wants to think about what to wear to a funeral or a memorial service, it's important that you know how to put together an appropriate outfit for these events. Unlike just about every other social situation in this book, this is one time when you don't want to stand out in any way or draw attention to yourself with a fashion-forward silhouette, interesting pair of shoes, or trendy beauty look. ***The goal is to create an outfit that befits the occasion, via a dark color palette and conservatively cut clothing.*** Stick to the basics: a modest black dress and heels will always work. You can also wear navy or a very dark gray, but anything else is inappropriate.

In addition to the color restrictions, remember to pick timeless pieces with minimalist sensibilities; an embellished jacket or a ruffled skirt are not right for this occasion, even if they're black. This is not a time to show skin, so opt for ensembles with prim necklines and longer hemlines. An ideal dress would come up to your collarbone, down to your knee, and have sleeves.

Speaking of which, if you must wear something sleeveless—which is not recommended—make sure you

OTHER OUTFIT
IDEAS

1 black slacks + navy blouse + black blazer

2 black maxi skirt + black silk shell + black cardigan

3 charcoal pencil skirt + black blouse + black blazer

4 black shift dress + black opaque tights + dark gray cardigan

5 navy long-sleeve dress + black pumps + dark sunglasses

GO FOR

black dresses with high necklines; simple black or charcoal pumps with a modest heel; dark sunglasses

STEER CLEAR

colors; prints and patterns; overly embellished or textured garments; miniskirts; body-con dresses; flats; statement jewelry

RISKY BUSINESS

hats (possibly appropriate if the entire occasion is taking place outside with people who tend to dress more formally. In this case, go for a simple black shape; otherwise it's simply too attention grabbing and apply some extra sunscreen instead.)

"Stick to the BASICS: A MODEST BLACK dress and heels will always work."

wear a wrap or jacket for the ceremony itself. As far as accessories go, sunglasses are acceptable, but hats are a little too attention-grabbing in our opinion.

Katherine went for a long-sleeve dress with a high neckline and chiffon sleeves for this situation. Though the sleeves are slightly sheer, they're balanced by the dress's modest cut. She added a caramel pair of sunglasses, which work because they lighten up her outfit a touch and look less severe than a black pair. For her shoes, she selected a simple pair of black heels with subtle woven detailing, which makes them on-point for daytime.

Hillary also opted for a dress and selected a simple A-line style with elbow-length sleeves. The dress is made from heavy brocade, which means it is a bit more formal. She picked a basic pair of black heels and an understated ladylike frame bag to finish the look.

SPORTING EVENT

Just like the game itself, there are lots of variables in play when getting dressed for a sporting event. To ensure that you keep your competitive edge—style-wise, of course—it's important to figure out as many details about the event as possible. Are you seeing a pro game or are you heading to a college campus? What's the venue like: are you going to be inside a giant sports center or outside in a stadium? Obviously it's also important to consider the forecast, season, and expected duration of the game—all things that can influence your outfit. *The goal is to create an outfit that takes all of these factors into consideration, while still showing who you are in an understated way.*

Once you've sorted out all the necessary bits of info, the first thing to consider is your footwear. There will be walking involved—through the parking lot, in the stadium, to the concession stands—so make sure your shoes can go the distance and work on stairs, too. If you want to wear shoes with some heel height (we're guilty of this charge) and there's any chance you might be on grass, go for a wedge. In addition to being a sturdier choice in general, wedges are always better for navigating on turf and look less formal. As far as your clothes, it probably goes without saying that you should stick to heartier, durable materials like denim and cotton; this is not a time to break out your delicate linens or anything irreplaceable. It's always a good idea to make sure your outfit includes lightweight layers, too, as the temperature

can vary a great deal over the course of a game.

One fashionable way to tackle this social situation is to look for pieces that are made from casual materials but with a body-skimming silhouette. For a nighttime basketball game, Katherine picked a heather gray sweatshirt skirt for the base of her look because it's cute while nodding to the athletic theme of the evening. She added a couple of layers on top—a striped tank and a thin cashmere turtleneck sweater, which she can easily remove if necessary. To ensure she doesn't freeze from the air-conditioning, she added a pair of darker gray tights that coordinate with her gray lace-up booties. Then, to pull the entire look together, she added a cute cropped jacket and a versatile leather bag.

Hillary went for a more casual look for her sporting event—a college football game—and picked her favorite pair of worn-in bell-bottom jeans as the base of her look. She chose a long-sleeve striped t-shirt, which she tucked in to give the outfit a slightly more feminine silhouette, and then added a suede jacket in a lovely honey color. Her outerwear might seem slightly fancy for this occasion, but it is cut like a denim jacket, which makes it a less dressy pick. For accessories she opted for a black knit beanie to keep her head warm, a long-strap bag, and a bright red oversized scarf along too. The finishing touches came from a sturdy pair of dark gray wedges and a cozy pair of nubby knit socks.

"
THE FIRST thing to consider is your *FOOTWEAR.*
"

OTHER OUTFIT IDEAS

1 lightweight cotton skirt + racer back tank top + low-top sneakers

2 relaxed, cuffed chinos + semi-sheer tank + flip-flops

3 wide-leg shorts + graphic print t-shirt + low wedges + denim jacket

4 cropped chunky-knit cardigan + draped t-shirt + skinny jeans + flat ankle boots

GO FOR

COLD WEATHER: sporty fabrics and prints like stripes and heather gray; cropped cashmere sweaters; motorcycle jackets; long-sleeve t-shirts; your favorite jeans; wedge boots; motorcycle boots; thick tights; beanies, berets, and other wool hats

WARM WEATHER: soft cotton layers; lightweight cardigans; cuffed denim shorts; slouchy khaki or cargo shorts; cropped trench coats; cotton sundresses; flat sandals or moccasins; low-top canvas sneakers

STEER CLEAR

short skirts; sweats; waist belts; body-con dresses; strappy tops or dresses; pumps; clutch bags; nighttime makeup

RISKY BUSINESS

heels (please opt for wedges or heeled boots if you must)

THEATER & PLAYHOUSE

The GOAL is to create a moderately dressy outfit that has at least ONE dramatic or standout element.

It doesn't matter if you're a show-tune crooner or a very serious dramatist; when the theater calls, you'd better answer—wearing something sharp, of course. After all, theatrics are literally the name of the game at the playhouse, so looking on-point is practically a requirement! Of course, much like the Opera, how dressed up you get for the theater depends on your location and the time of the show.

The goal is to create a moderately dressy outfit that has at least one dramatic or standout element. If you're going to an evening performance in a larger city, you'll want to wear something that's at least as formal as what you'd wear on a First Date to a nice restaurant. If the show is a matinee, opt for something similar to what you'd select for a Ladies' Luncheon. Just remember that you'll be inside in air-conditioning, so bring an extra layer of outerwear, like a cardigan or a trench.

Ideally you should put together an ensemble that has some personality. That means you can wear something that's a little quirky or has a lot of flair—you are going to be surrounded by people who support the arts, after all. Bearing that in mind, this is an excellent time to try out a look that involves mixed prints, a dress in an unusual color or with unique details, or a fashion-forward silhouette. Just make sure that whatever you pick is comfortable when you sit down and doesn't involve a hat; no one wants his or her view blocked by your chapeau. Also, do us a favor and skip the jeans please. There are so many times when denim

is appropriate, but we're asking you to step it up a notch for this occasion.

For Katherine's theater look, she decided to take this opportunity to play with prints—one of her favorite style tricks—which can look super-chic when done right. She started with a draped leopard mini dress and then cinched it in at the waist with a skinny belt. (A skinny belt is a great option for girls with short waists, just make sure it's less than two inches thick.) She added an unstructured, faded linen leopard coat for a little contrast. Instead of wearing pumps, she selected a pair of lace-up booties that are appropriate for day or night. The ankle boots are a slightly safer choice than pumps, in that they're a bit more casual, so Katherine won't feel overdone. Finally, she accessorized with a trendy black clutch in a larger size, a choice that's just as versatile as her shoes.

Hillary decided to break out one of her favorite vintage dresses for this occasion. The frock's pretty green color and hand-painted print are both noteworthy, while the full skirt and elbow-length sleeves are comfortable and warm. Since the dress does have a fair amount going on, she added a slim white belt to break up the expanse of color and pattern and give her whole look an extra dose of polish. For the finishing touches, she selected a cork clutch and a pair of chocolate brown cutout-detailed pumps, as both pieces are appropriate for day.

STYLE SUGGESTION

The key to mixing prints is to choose two patterns with similar color tones or use one black-and-white print paired with a colorful one. Generally, it's best to mix two small prints. However sometimes mixing a larger colorful print with a tiny neutral print (like black and white or black and tan) can work too.

OTHER OUTFIT IDEAS

1. print pants + silk tank + cardigan

2. pencil skirt + patterned blouse + casual cropped blazer

3. black harem pants + metallic tank + shrunken denim jacket + vibrant lips

4. slip dress + cropped embellished jacket + oxfords

5. cowl-neck sweater dress + dark opaque tights + lace-up ankle boots

GO FOR

mixed prints; trench coats; fifties-style day dresses; pencil skirts; patterned blouses; carrot trousers; cropped pants; lightweight blazers; sophisticated trousers; ankle booties; animal-print pumps; wedges; oversized clutches; long vintage necklaces

STEER CLEAR

jeans; sweats; hats

RISKY BUSINESS

sleeveless or tank styles (always remember to bring a sweater or jacket to keep warm in the air-conditioned theater)

TRAVELING

Oh the horrors of traveling! We don't even mean the planes—though they are rather gross for the most part—what offends our eyes are our fellow travelers. While we certainly don't suggest a return to the old days, when plane travel was an exotic treat that called for dressing up, there has to be something else for people to wear besides velour tracksuits, pseudo sweatpants, and other similarly sloppy ensembles. Wait, there is! In fact, marvelous options abound that are just as easy and just as cozy as these aforementioned absurdities. *The goal is to create a relaxed outfit that looks put together, but is secretly as comfortable as your pajamas.* Your ensemble also needs to be uncomplicated, so that you can breeze through security in seconds.

Whether you're on vacation or heading somewhere for work, the most important travel tip is to wear a number of lightweight layers. By having these easy-to-remove layers, you're ensuring that no matter how hot or cold the plane may be, you can adapt and stay comfortable. Much like on a Road Trip, always opt for natural fabrics (cotton, denim) in dark neutral colors and stay away from anything that's dry-clean only or ultra-delicate (it will wrinkle in seconds). Pick foot-friendly shoes that allow you to walk long distances, and make sure they're a style that slips on and off easily. We prefer to wear footwear that also requires socks so we don't have to put our bare feet on the airport floor, but we're a bit particular like that. Other ne-cessities: sunglasses to mask your tired or dry eyes, a lightweight scarf which can double as a pillow, and a roomy handbag that can store all your in-flight necessities.

If you have a red-eye flight and have to go directly to work the next day, or simply like to look polished on a plane, take a cue from Hillary's travel outfit. She started with a super-soft pair of stretchy jeans in a dark wash—they always look crisp, even though they're as cozy as leggings—then added a simple bright t-shirt for a little pop of color. The key to her outfit is the trench coat: it barely matters what she's wearing underneath it because the trench pulls everything together and makes her look sleek and sophisticated. To make security a cinch, Hillary opted for a gray pair of slip-on ankle boots, then accessorized with a roomy tote, pale pink cashmere scarf, and a sharp pair of sunglasses.

Katherine, on the other hand, went for a more downtown look, which is centered on a pair of black leggings and a handful of soft tops. First she put on a charcoal sweater as the base of her look, and then added a denim button-down and a thin gray cardigan over the shirt. Per our wardrobe rules, she accessorized with a large soft scarf, boots that are easy-on, easy-off, and an oversized pair of shades. Finally, Katherine grabbed a big bag with a long strap, which she can wear across her body for additional security and hands-free traveling.

OTHER OUTFIT
IDEAS

1 striped cardigan + black t-shirt + slouchy cuffed jeans + canvas low-top sneakers

2 skinny stretchy black jeans + white tank + semi-sheer v-neck sweater + low motorcycle boots

3 dark cotton maxi skirt + layered drapey t-shirts

GO FOR

lightweight layers; comfortable jeans with stretch; dark wash or black denim; trench coats; dark neutrals; machine-washable fabrics; cardigans; denim shirts; comfy t-shirts; sunglasses; roomy totes; easily removed boots or ankle booties; moccasins or ballet flats; across-body bags; beanies

STEER CLEAR

delicate fabrics; dry-clean–only pieces; light colors; heavy jackets or sweaters (better to go for easily removed layers); tight jeans without stretch; flip-flops; short skirts; tailored blazers or trousers; shorts

RISKY BUSINESS

sundresses (can be hard to layer); hats (a hat without a back brim, like a newsboy cap, can work; otherwise it's annoying); maxi skirts (it's fine if you're wearing one with a slightly narrow silhouette, but a voluminous peasant skirt can take up too much space)

_W_EDDING BLACK-TIE

The GOAL is to create a memorable outfit that addresses the formality of the event.

Of all the nuptial options, our favorite is also the least common: the black-tie wedding. After all, in your post-prom years, how many opportunities do you really get to go all out and wear a truly formal dress? Naturally, the scarcity of these full-tilt fancy occasions means that they're also a bit challenging to address. The goal is to create a memorable outfit that addresses the formality of the event. The black-tie wedding definitely calls for a dress—usually a long gown—which requires some degree of investment. Of course, no one wants to spend their nest egg on some big _Gone with the Wind_ confection they can only wear once, so what's a girl to do? Two words: get resourceful.

Our favorite way to get a great gown without

> **"** _As for all weddings, stay away from anything that's even remotely white or close to white in tone..._ **"**

blowing all of our savings is to go vintage. No matter where you live, there has to be an amazing designer vintage or resale store in your area. There are a couple of reasons to go vintage: you're guaranteed no one else will have your dress and you can have it tailored to your body, ensuring a perfect fit.

If, for some reason, you don't have a go-to resource in your area, there are loads of lovely vintage e-tailers online, too. It might seem scary to buy something like this via the web, but if you know your (very accurate) measurements and buy a size or two larger than you might normally wear, you should be more than fine. Remember: it's always easy to take something in, but too small is harder to fix. If you'd rather not sleuth

OTHER OUTFIT
IDEAS

1 dark metallic one-shoulder dress + jet beaded clutch + satin d'orsay heels

2 jewel-tone silk-chiffon strapless gown + chunky rhinestone bib necklace + miniature metallic clutch

3 solid-colored embellished vintage gown + black wrap + modern jewelry

4 full-skirt, knee-length organza dress + glittery stilettos + sleek topknot

5 slim black maxi dress + black faux fur gilet + satin stilettos

" Our FAVORITE way to get a GREAT GOWN without blowing all of our savings is to go VINTAGE. "

GO FOR

long, solid-colored gowns; metallic one-shoulder dresses; short black dresses with strong silhouettes; faux fur vests, jackets, and shrugs; embellished trophy jackets; fancy feminine heels (stiletto heels with embellishments, satin, or sparkle); small evening clutches; structured evening bags; multiple pieces of clear-stone costume or fine jewelry; black sheer or swiss dot tights for the colder months; high topknot updos; strong red lips or strong cat eyeliner; well-manicured hands and feet

STEER CLEAR

casual fabrics; animal prints; red dresses; white dresses (including cream, ivory, pale gold, nude); mini dresses; long dresses in bold prints; blazers; cardigans; chunky heels; day bags

RISKY BUSINESS

prints (this can work if the prints are dark and or muted); short dresses (make sure they are formal enough)

the shops, you can always hit up your best pals and raid their closets instead.

As far as selecting the actual dress, as for all weddings, stay away from anything that's even remotely white or close to white in tone, which means no beige, ivory, nude, champagne, or even pale silver. Since black-tie weddings typically call for long gowns, we also suggest staying away from patterned styles, which will just look busy in photographs. Instead look to deep jewel tones or dark neutrals like black, brown, navy, or gray. If you prefer a metallic gown, make sure it's a rich color like pewter, copper, or gunmetal—lighter metallics can look cheap.

You can also consider a shorter dress. Yes, it's a little riskier, but it can be done in a wholly appropriate way. First, remember that short doesn't mean micro, so make sure the hemline is at least mid-thigh in length. Then, simply consider the following items and you'll be fine: fabric, flair, and footwear. Regarding fabric, it's imperative that you pick a very formal material— silk, crepe, chiffon, georgette, or some combination like silk-chiffon or satin-crepe—to offset the shorter hemline.

> ❝ *Finally, your shoes: think formal and feminine high heels that are either embellished (feathers, stones, sparkle), made out of a dressy fabric, like satin, or both!* ❞

Next, you need to add some flair and dressiness via jewelry; rhinestones are always a good idea— just make sure that you've picked rich-looking costume jewelry with lots of stones and shine. Finally, your shoes: think formal and feminine high heels that are either embellished (feathers, stones, sparkle), made out of a dressy fabric (like satin), or both! While your grandmother might protest, hosiery is not a necessity; these days it's merely an option. That said, if you are putting your gams on display, make sure they're toned, free of imperfections (like bruises), and have a healthy glow (break out the body bronzer or faux tanner).

Bearing all of this in mind, we decided to give you two distinctly different options for a black-tie wedding. As a thoroughly modern woman, Katherine opted for a shorter dress: she's more comfortable in a higher hemline, and it just fits with her personal style better. Accordingly, she picked a full-skirted halter dress that hits just above knee level; anything higher would border on the too-casual side of things. In addition to its voluminous silhouette, the dress is accented by some structured ruffle detailing, which amplifies its formality. Per our earlier tip, Katherine also added loads of gorgeous rhinestone jewelry in the form of earrings, numerous bracelets, and an oversized ring. Since the dress and jewelry are such standouts, she kept the rest of her accessories relatively subtle, opting for a black patent clutch and a pair of glittery, pointy pumps with a super-slim heel. (A stiletto always looks more formal than a chunky heel.) Finally, a note about Katherine's beauty look: instead of wearing her hair down, which would compete with her dramatic halter dress, she balanced things by going for a slicked-back bun instead.

Hillary, on the other hand, loves a long gown, so she picked a stunning strapless style for this social occasion. While the lines of her dress are quite timeless, the rich chocolate brown color is very unexpected, as is the textured detailing at the neckline and hem. These small tweaks make the dress more modern, while still letting its classically romantic look shine through. Thanks to the textured bodice, Hillary decided to forgo a necklace and opted for chunky drop earrings and an oversized ring instead. Metallics are always a chic way to accent neutrals, so she picked a small, structured gold clutch and metallic nail polish to complement the gown.

Wedding: COCKTAIL

It's time to celebrate! Why, you might ask? Well that's easy: you're going to a wedding that calls for cocktail attire, and that's the easiest kind—outfit-wise, of course. While you have restrictions due to the formality of a black-tie event and daytime nuptials require certain practical considerations, the early evening wedding—oftentimes labeled semiformal, formal, or black-tie optional—is a bit more flexible. *The goal is to create an outfit that is similar to what you'd wear to a fancy cocktail party.* These weddings are more festive, so you can wear your favorite party dress—as long as it's not white.

The wonderful thing about this social situation is that you are allowed to break out a fun frock and wear some of your more outrageous accessories if you want. Due to the earlier hour, we suggest sticking to shorter dresses, but feel free to try out a bold color or on-trend silhouette: it's perfectly fine to have a little fun with your fashion choices. As always, you need to stay away from all colors in the white family, and while some people say red is now okay at all weddings, we think it is risky.

For a summer wedding, Katherine picked a strapless dress with a spirited polka-dot print and a pretty peplum. To add a little formality and personality to her outfit, she opted for eye-catching accessories, including bright red lipstick and loads of gold bracelets on each wrist. Since the dress has a more elaborate silhouette, she kept her shoes simple—classic black pointy pumps—then finished her outfit with an unusual gold seashell clutch.

Hillary decided to create a look that would be appropriate for a fall or winter wedding, so she started with a sleek black dress with lace details. The asymmetrical sleeves, semitransparent neckline, and hemline trim all elevate the frock's simple silhouette and make it much more interesting and delicate. She added classic matte black tights to ward off the chill and a dance-floor–ready pair of platform pumps. Finally she incorporated a little glitz into her look via an oversized pair of rhinestone earrings, a sparkly bracelet, and a black patent clutch.

> **SIDE NOTE :** *Don't let anyone tell you that you have to wear hosiery—we're beyond that now. But if you want to add warmth or extra coverage to your look, try sheer black stockings or a pair of swiss-dot stockings. (Sheer hosiery is always dressier than opaque.)*

STYLE SUGGESTION

The most versatile dress to invest in for weddings is a solid-color strapless dress that hits approximately 2 to 4 inches above the top of you knee. You can dress it up or down, make it appropriate for any season, and give it a total makeover by updating your accessories and outerwear. Black is swell, of course, but jewel-tone hues like navy or a vibrant green are great, too. Make sure it's in a dressy fabric—no cotton jersey!—and that you add a shoulder-covering accent, like a wrap, bolero, or other cropped jacket.

"These weddings are MORE FESTIVE, so you can wear your favorite party dress!"

GO FOR

cocktail dresses in fun prints or bright colors; dresses with interesting materials or textures; platform pumps or strappy sandals; metallic or patent clutches; black or swiss-dot tights in colder months; oversized bracelets; rhinestone jewelry

STEER CLEAR

daytime materials like cotton jersey or denim; white dresses or anything in that color family; print dresses that involve lots of red or white; long gowns with full skirts or sequins (save that for black-tie); blazers; cardigans; day bags

RISKY BUSINESS

animal prints (a dark animal print will work for a creative or fashionable crowd, but if your crew is even remotely conservative, skip them all together); skirt-and-blouse combos (if it's fancy enough, you might be able to make it work, but this is really an occasion for dresses); red dresses (can be lovely but don't wear something too attention grabbing; go for a shorter hemline and a modest neckline)

RELIGIOUS OCCASION: NIGHT—PG. 110

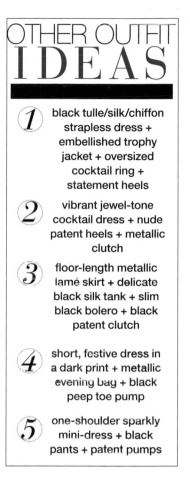

OTHER OUTFIT
IDEAS

1 black tulle/silk/chiffon strapless dress + embellished trophy jacket + oversized cocktail ring + statement heels

2 vibrant jewel-tone cocktail dress + nude patent heels + metallic clutch

3 floor-length metallic lamé skirt + delicate black silk tank + slim black bolero + black patent clutch

4 short, festive dress in a dark print + metallic evening bag + black peep toe pump

5 one-shoulder sparkly mini-dress + black pants + patent pumps

> *We suggest STICKING to SHORTER dresses, but feel free to try out a BOLD color or ON-TREND silhouette.*

Wedding: DAYTIME

The goal is to create an outfit that's cheerful and celebratory, ideally something similar to what you'd wear to a Daytime Religious Occasion—but DRESSIER.

The third installment in our wedding trifecta is also the most casual—the daytime wedding. But just because the ceremony and celebration take place in the (hopefully) sunshine, don't make the mistake of thinking you can turn up in any old thing. In fact, this type of wedding has thrown many otherwise stylish ladies for a loop! The goal is to create an outfit that's cheerful and celebratory, ideally something similar to what you'd wear to a Daytime Religious Occasion—but dressier. As always, you should never wear a white dress (this includes cream, ecru, and even nude), and avoiding white-heavy prints (our rule is the print cannot be 50% white or more) is imperative, too!

Much like at a Black-Tie Wedding, the trick to getting your daytime wedding look right is really paying attention to your choice of materials.

Avoid super-casual fabrics at all costs, meaning no jersey, cotton, or polyester; instead, reach for lightweight dressy fabrics like chiffon or silk, as they will give you the right hint of formality.

Picking the appropriate footwear is of paramount importance, too, especially if the wedding is taking place outdoors on the grass or sand. The best way to navigate nature is to go for a wedge; stilettos, with their ground-puncturing skinny heels, are a perilous choice. Of course, if the day doesn't call for such adventures, you're free to wear a range of shoe styles. Nude pumps are always at the top of our list—they're flattering and will make most party dresses feel more appropriate for day—but an embellished flat sandal can work, too, especially if paired with an exotic-print maxi dress for a beach wedding.

" REACH for lightweight dressy fabrics like CHIFFON or SILK, as they will give you the right hint of FORMALITY. "

" *Take your time selecting the right sunglasses; nothing makes us crazier than seeing someone in a lovely dress and sporty shades—ew!* "

Last, but certainly not least, please take your time selecting the right sunglasses to go with your ensemble. Nothing makes us crazier than seeing someone in a lovely dress and sporty shades—ew! Skip the super-trendy or athletic styles and pick a ladylike pair that complements your dress in a chic way.

The lovely thing about the daytime wedding is that all hemlines (save micro mini) are equally appropriate. Katherine, for example, chose a long dress with a gray abstract print and a slightly bohemian vibe. To dress it up a bit and make it more appropriate for the occasion, she added a silver rope-style belt and a pair of dangly silver earrings, two details that definitely elevate her look. As for her shoes, Katherine selected a comfortable pair of gray leather wedges, which are easy to walk in and give her a little height, too. Instead of picking a small, structured, sparkly handbag—which reads "evening"—she grabbed an oversized ivory clutch, which is perfect for daytime.

Hillary wanted to wear something a bit brighter, so she opted for an above-the-knee strapless dress in a vibrant fuchsia print. (Bold prints typically look best on shorter frocks; they can get a bit overwhelming on a floor-length frock.) Since the dress is so bright, she kept the rest of her ensemble relatively subtle with nude pumps, a cork clutch, and a pale pink shawl. Of course, no outfit would be complete without a personal touch or two, so she added a yellow vintage bracelet for an unexpected accent and some neutral sunglasses to finish her look.

SIDE NOTE: *Generally speaking, it's better to stick to cheerful colors for daytime weddings, think: light and bright. That said, you certainly can wear black—especially if the wedding starts in early- to mid-afternoon and goes into the evening—just make sure your fabric is appropriate and add color via your accessories. Again, nude pumps would be perfect for this occasion, especially if paired with a vibrant or print clutch.*

OTHER OUTFIT
IDEAS

1. sorbet-colored grecian dress + tan wedges + gold clutch

2. silk slip dress + nude strappy heels + antique pendant necklace

3. solid maxi dress + brown leather belt + embellished flat sandals + snake print clutch

GO FOR

light or bright colors; dressy daytime fabrics (like silk or chiffon); maxi dresses (either solid or in a neutral print); exotic-print cocktail dresses; bright or bold party dresses; vintage-inspired dresses; skirt suits (in light or bright colors); cropped jackets; lace boleros; trench coats; nude pumps; dressy flat sandals; oversized clutches (in pale colors or light neutrals); colorful shawls; oversized sunglasses

STEER CLEAR

white; casual fabrics (cotton, linen, jersey, polyester); denim; super-short hemlines; any heels you'd wear to a nightclub; ballet flats (unless you are under 16 or very pregnant; in either case, make sure they're embellished); tiny, glittery evening bags; wraparound/sporty sunglasses

RISKY BUSINESS

black (see Side Note)

WEEKEND

You know that old saying about how you can tell how talented a chef is based on how well they cook a single egg? That idea—the simplest stuff is always the hardest—is true for getting dressed, too. No wonder assembling cute weekend-casual outfits feels so tricky: it's one of the few social situations that seem to be free from wardrobe rules. In addition to this laissez-faire attitude, the other tricky bit about Saturday/Sunday ensembles is the fact that you shouldn't use any go-to pieces from your regular week. Confusing? And how! The goal is to create an effortlessly chic outfit that is undoubtedly casual, but still feels pulled together.

While during the week you must create a casual outfit with a little polish (see Errands for more details on why and how), when the weekend rolls around, you can and should go for comfort. We have one simple rule: if it has to be dry-cleaned, it's probably not right for a casual weekend look. That said, you still want to look cute, so our way of tackling that is to pick one trendy piece that's appropriate for your off-duty hours—like a straw fedora, of-the-moment jean, or the season's hottest sandal style—and use that as the jumping-off point. Now, don't take this as an invitation to pile on all the casual, au courant items you've ever wanted to try! Be specific and stick to one piece, maybe two if you must, to save yourself from looking like a victim. Remember: the key to looking effortless is editing!

For Hillary's easy-breezy look, she picked a black jersey maxi skirt as the foundation of her outfit. This is one of the few times the soft material is perfectly appropriate (it's overused, to our taste) because it offers the ease of sweats but with more style. Next she added two lightweight cotton layers: a simple black-and-white graphic t-shirt and an army green field jacket with a drawstring waist. Again, as mentioned for the Rain or a Road Trip, a loose semi-long jacket is always more flattering if you can cinch it in at the waist in some way. To add some visual texture to the look, Hillary added a lightweight print scarf and a pair of gray flat boots, and then finished things off with an oversized leather across-body bag and a classic pair of sunglasses.

> ## *"The GOAL is to create an effortlessly chic outfit that is undoubtedly casual, but still feels pulled together."*

Katherine opted for an equally low-fuss, high-impact look, starting with a cotton menswear-style button-up shirt, which is a great go-to for the weekend. This shirt will work with loads of options—skinny jeans, denim shorts, relaxed and cuffed khakis—especially when styled with the sleeves rolled up and scrunched. However, this weekend she decided to wear it with a pair of distressed overalls for ultimate comfort. Katherine cuffed the overalls to give them a more purposeful "boyfriend" look and added a chic trench, too. The trick with overalls is to remember that they're inherently juvenile, so be sure to balance them with more grown-up elements. As for her footwear, she picked some simple cutout oxfords, but basic sandals, ballet flats, moccasins, or loafers would work just as well. Finally, she grabbed a tan leather flap shoulder bag with a chain strap that she chose to carry as an oversized clutch. It makes the bag feel less precious, plus it's a cute trick if you don't want to swap the contents of the bag you used the night before.

OTHER OUTFIT IDEAS

1. stretchy skinny jeans + worn-in t-shirt + field jacket + low motorcycle boots
2. oversized cotton button-up + cuffed denim shorts + brown leather woven belt + moccasins
3. simple sundress + denim jacket + flat sandals + straw fedora

GO FOR

machine-washable fabrics; daytime-appropriate fabrics like cotton, denim, and jersey; tank tops; t-shirts; skinny jeans with stretch; chambray skirts or shirtdresses; denim shorts or cutoffs; cuffed khakis, cargos, or jeans; maxi skirts; button-ups; denim jackets; army jackets; flannel workshirts; trench coats; moccasins; ballet flats; flat boots; sandals; oxfords; canvas low-top lace-ups; slouchy bags; across-body bags; print scarves; sunglasses

STEER CLEAR

dry-clean-only fabrics; leather; sequins or metallics; body-con clothing; miniskirts or short shorts; heels or platforms; heavy eye makeup

RISKY BUSINESS

skinny jeans (make sure they have stretch in them); wedges

HILLARY & KATHERINE'S WARDROBE ESSENTIALS

Chefs might daydream about the perfect meal, while musicians make ever-changing lists of their five favorite songs, but for clothing aficionados like us, it's all about the perfect wardrobe. We can spend hours editing these key pieces—weighing the merits of one must-have jacket against another, determining which hardworking pieces are absolute essentials. But don't think this is just some mindless game we play to pass the time: by understanding what you have and what you need, you can build a much better wardrobe!

That said, when you go through this book, we suggest that you create your own version of this exercise. Remember, there's not a single foolproof, flawless solution to this riddle: your answers might look very different from ours—which is good! They should be very specifically tailored and personalized, as these selections reflect your personal style, body type, and age.

As you go through the different style situations, ask yourself, "What would I wear to this event?" and be sure to jot down your responses. Let's say you end up writing "leopard heels" or "classic trench" or "slim black skirt" as the answer for fifteen social occasions. Clearly that tells you something: you could wear this piece over and over again to loads of different events. Bearing that in mind, wouldn't it be smart to invest in an amazing version of said item? Indeed! So take that clothing clue and use it to shape your future shopping plans in a very smart way.

Hillary's Wardrobe Essentials

Slim Black Blazer

Tan Wedges

Aviator Sunglasses

Shrunken Jean Jacket

A-Line Structured Dress

Neutral Clutch

Black Skinny Jeans

Coral Lipstick

Nude Pumps

Silky Print Blouse

Field
Jacket

Black
Party Skirt

Lace Dress

Peep-Toc Heels

Black
Strapless Dress

Gray
Pencil Skirt

Trench
Coat

Dark Flare
Jeans

Gray
Handbag

Solid
Silky Shell

Katherine's Wardrobe Essentials

Neutral-Colored T-Shirts

Black Body-Con Dress

Animal-Print Clutch

Thin Brown Belt

Black Leather Moto Jacket

Red Nail Polish

RGB

Dark Skinny Jeans

Black Ankle Boots

Men's Style Watch

Short Flippy Skirt

Print Scarf

Cropped Trench

Menswear-Inspired Flats

Gray Heels

Breton-Stripe Sweater

Gray Cardigan

Slim Black Pants

Big Black Day Bag

Denim Shorts

Pink Lipgloss

OUTFIT INDEX

ART GALLERY

Hillary
Mason top
J Brand jeans
Banana Republic hat
Yarnz scarf
Chan Luu necklace
Virgins, Saints, & Angels necklace
CC Skye necklace
Virgins, Saints, & Angels cuff
Forever 21 purse
W3 black buckle booties

Katherine
Ulla Johnson jacket
Elizabeth and James blouse
Laeken skirt
Alyssa Norton bracelet
Rebecca Minkoff bag
W3 black lace-up booties

BARBECUE

Hillary
Ecote at Urban Outfitters jacket
Love Sam top
Kasil shorts
Zimmermann bikini
Chan Luu bracelet
Ray-Ban sunglasses
Cole Haan purse
W3 denim espadrille wedges

Katherine
Rachel Comey top
Jenni Kayne shorts
Levi's jacket
Chloe sunglasses
Rebecca Minkoff purse
W3 silver and black t-strap sandals

BEACH & POOL

Hillary
Lotta Stensson caftan
Shimmi bikini
Forever 21 hat
Vintage turquoise necklace
Louis Vuitton tote
W3 chain-detail sandals

Katherine
Eres bathing suit
Corpus shirt
J. Crew shorts
Nordstrom hat
Benjamin sunglasses
Chan Luu bracelet
Lotta Stensson bag
W3 tan woven flat sandals

BENEFIT & FUND-RAISER

Hillary
Gr. Dano dress
Smythe trench coat
Topshop necklace
Vintage Ferragamo purse
W3 brown cutout pumps

Katherine
Acne dress
Trina Turk necklace
Miu Miu clutch
W3 yellow snake print peep-toe pumps

BIRTHDAY PARTY

Hillary
3.1 Phillip Lim dress
Rachel Leigh earrings
Ami bangles
Arianne Tunney clutch
W3 nude pump

Katherine
Katy Rodriguez dress
Simone jacket
Forever 21 bracelet
Noir bracelet
Givenchy clutch
W3 black sparkle pumps

BOWLING (& OTHER ACTIVITIES)

Hillary
Rebecca Minkoff jacket
291 tank
J Brand pants
Bowling Bag (Prop)
W3 denim espadrille wedges

Katherine
Steven Alan shirt
Inhabit sweater
The Row jeans
Chanel purse
W3 sneakers

COCKTAIL PARTY: CORPORATE

Hillary
Vintage blouse
Staerk skirt
Jack Rabbit Collection belt
A.P.C. bag
W3 black platform peep-toe pumps

Katherine
Camilla and Marc jacket
Shakuhachi dress
House of Lavande necklace
Givenchy clutch
W3 black sparkle pumps

COCKTAIL PARTY: FESTIVE

Hillary
Vintage dress
Joie jacket
Temperley London clutch
W3 black platform peep-toe pumps

Katherine
Twelfth Street by Cynthia Vincent top
Rag & Bone pants
Bing Bang earrings
House of Lavande necklace
Perrin Paris clutch
W3 black sparkle pumps

COLD WEATHER

Hillary
H&M shirt
Calypso cardigan
Mason jacket
7 For All Mankind jeans
Jennifer Ouellette hat
Gap belt
H&M gloves
Forever 21 socks
Cole Haan bag
W3 tan wedges

Katherine
Mike Gonzalez coat
Jenni Kayne jacket
Inhabit sweater
H&M shorts
Suzi Roher belt
Jennifer Ouellette hat
Vintage gloves from The Way We Wore
Marni bracelet
Donna Karan tights
Marni bag
W3 black buckle booties

CONCERT

Hillary
Rebecca Minkoff jacket
Elizabeth and James top
Joie tank
J Brand jeans
Las ring
Veda purse
W3 black sparkle pumps

Katherine
All Saints top
Topshop vest
Muubaa skirt
Linea Pelle belt
Jennifer Elizabeth necklace
Rebecca Minkoff bag
W3 black buckle booties

COUNTRY CLUB

Hillary
Oscar de la Renta cardigan
Oscar de la Renta top
Opening Ceremony skirt
Benjamin sunglasses
Banana Republic belt
Lia Sophia bracelet
JJ Winters clutch
W3 denim espadrille wedges

Katherine
Juicy Couture trench coat
Wren top
Rachel Comey shorts
Hat Attack fedora
Elegantly Waisted belt
Kate Spade purse
W3 tan wedges

COURTROOM

Hillary
Vintage dress
Burberry coat
Topshop belt
Forever 21 earrings
Cartier watch
Rebecca Minkoff purse
W3 black cutout pumps

Katherine
Rachel Comey jacket
Bebe shirt
Club Monaco pants
Benjamin sunglasses
Melinda Maria bracelet
Karen Zambos bag
W3 gray pumps

DATE: CASUAL

Hillary
Barlow jacket
Rebecca Taylor top
Genetic Denim jeans
Bing Bang necklace
Chloe bag
W3 denim espadrille wedges

Katherine
Banana Republic cardigan
Pins and Needles dress
Vita bracelet
Forever 21 socks
Vintage Gucci bag
W3 tan wedges

DATE: FIRST

Hillary
Tibi tank
DKNY coat
3.1 Phillip Lim skirt
Linea Pelle belt
Hue tights
Romy Gold clutch
W3 black platform peep-toe pumps

Katherine
Chloe jacket
Alternative Apparel tee
Dallin Chase skirt
Bing Bang bracelet
Givenchy clutch
W3 black lace-up booties

DINNER PARTY

Hillary
All Saints dress
Rebecca Minkoff jacket
Vintage Chanel belt
Vintage bracelet from The Way We Wore
Romy Gold clutch
W3 black cutout pumps

Katherine
Zadig & Voltaire cardigan
Rachel Comey top
291 tank
Rachel Comey pants
Bing Bang necklace
Topshop ring
JJ Winters purse
W3 gray lace-up boots

DOG PARK

Hillary
Ulla Johnson sweater
Genetic Denim jeans
Banana Republic hat
Bird purse
W3 gray flat ankle boots

Katherine
Simone jacket
G-Star Raw vest
Steven Alan top
Monrow pants
Vintage bracelet from The Way We Wore
W3 black wellies

ENGAGEMENT PARTY

Hillary
Vintage dress
Vintage clutch from The Way We Wore
W3 black platform peep-toe pumps

Katherine
Bruce jacket
Herve Leger dress
Noir ring
Melinda Maria bracelet
Bing Bang earrings
Banana Republic clutch
W3 nude pumps

ERRANDS

Hillary
Simone cardigan
291 tank
J Brand jeans
Alyssa Norton necklace
Cartier watch
Romy Gold purse
W3 denim espadrille wedges

Katherine
Simone jacket
Clu dress
Benjamin sunglasses
Deth Lauren necklace
Melinda Maria ring
Hermes purse
W3 black cutout lace-ups

FARMERS MARKET

Hillary
Vintage Albert Nipon dress
A.P.C. scarf
Madewell 1937 belt
Benjamin sunglasses
Perrin Paris purse
W3 multi-color beaded t-strap sandals

Katherine
Elizabeth and James shirt
J Brand pants
J. Crew hat
Vintage belt
Chan Luu bracelet
Madewell 1937 bag
W3 chain-detail sandals

FASHION EVENT

Hillary
Myne top
Chloe skirt
Vintage Missoni belt from The Way We Wore
CC Skye bracelet
Rachel Leigh earrings
Vintage Ferragamo purse
W3 yellow snake print peep-toe pumps

Katherine
Simone jacket
Vintage Levi's jacket
Alexx Jae & Milk t-shirt
Jenni Kayne skirt
House of Lavande necklace
Perrin Paris clutch
W3 black buckle booties

GAME NIGHT

Hillary
Winter Kate kimono
Joe's Jeans shirt
Genetic Denim jeans
Alyssa Norton necklace
Bird purse
W3 green snake print peep-toe pumps

Katherine
A.P.C. cardigan
Alternative Apparel tank
Loeffler Randall pants
Bing Bang necklace
Oliver Peoples glasses
L.L. Bean tote
W3 black zipper flats

GIRLS' NIGHT OUT

Hillary
Bebe dress
Marni earrings
Rebecca Minkoff bag
W3 neutral snake print pumps

Katherine
Dallin Chase vest
Bebe top
Jenni Kayne skirt
Alexander Wang bag
W3 black platform peep-toe pumps

GRADUATION

Hillary
Ulla Johnson dress
Elegantly Waisted belt
Skova bracelet
JJ Winters clutch
W3 tan wedges

Katherine
Raquel Allegra jacket
Adam top
Banana Republic Monogram pants
Benjamin sunglasses
Giles & Brother necklace
Vintage Gucci bag
W3 green snake print peep-toe pumps

JOB INTERVIEW: CONSERVATIVE

Hillary
Michael Kors jacket
Christian Dior pants
Yves Saint Laurent blouse
Yves Saint Laurent tote
W3 gray pumps

Katherine
J. Crew jacket
Iro top
Camilla and Marc skirt
H&M belt
Oliver Peoples glasses
Falke tights
La Mer Collection watch
Miu Miu bag
W3 black platform peep-toe pumps

JOB INTERVIEW: CREATIVE

Hillary
Vintage jacket
Staerk skirt
Suzi Roher belt
La Mer Collection watch
Mulberry bag
W3 black platform peep-toe pumps

Katherine
Tart bodysuit
Joie pants
Jenni Kayne belt
Giles & Brother necklace
Mulberry bag
W3 brown peep-toe pumps

KIDS' EVENT

Hillary
Alice + Olivia cardigan
Gemma top
Current/Elliott corduroys
Aldo necklace
Hobo purse
W3 gray wedges

Katherine
All Saints romper
Steven Alan shirt
A.P.C. belt
Forever 21 socks
Katherine's own bracelet combo
Ecote bag
W3 tan wedges

Riley
Bonpoint shirt
Stella McCartney for Gap jeans
Riley's own necklace and shoes

LADIES' LUNCHEON

Hillary
Oscar de la Renta top
Tracy Reese skirt
Burberry trench coat
Vintage bracelet
W3 yellow snake print peep-toe pumps

Katherine
Camilla and Marc jacket
H&M dress
Benjamin sunglasses
CC Skye bracelet
Perrin Paris bag
W3 nude pumps

MEET THE PARENTS

Hillary
Vintage Yves Saint Laurent blouse
Priorities cardigan
Rebecca Taylor skirt
Noir bracelet
Gucci bag
W3 nude pumps

Katherine
Chloe blouse
J Brand jeans
Vintage belt
Melinda Maria ring
Melinda Maria bracelet
Vintage Gucci bag
W3 tan wedges

MUSIC FESTIVAL

Hillary
Zimmermann dress
Vintage belt
Banana Republic hat
A.P.C. scarf
Chan Luu bracelets
Sharelli earrings
Hobo bag
W3 chain-detail sandals

Katherine
Smythe jacket
Topshop top
Kain tank
Vintage Levi's shorts
Benjamin sunglasses
Alyssa Norton necklace
Vintage scarf from The Way We Wore
Kimchi Blue purse
W3 black wellies

NEW YEAR'S EVE!

Hillary
Vintage dress from The Way We Wore
W3 black platform peep-toe pumps

Katherine
Vintage dress
Bebe stole
W3 black sparkle pumps

ON CAMERA

Hillary
Elizabeth and James jacket
Ulla Johnson top
Banana Republic skirt
W3 black platform peep-toe pumps

Katherine
Plastic Island top
H&M skirt
Vionnet belt
House of Harlow earrings
Giles & Brother cuff
Bing Bang ring
W3 nude pumps

OPERA

Hillary
Halston Heritage dress
Vintage stole from The Way We Wore
Elegantly Waisted belt
H&M necklace
Forever 21 bracelets
Banana Republic clutch
W3 black platform peep-toe pumps

Katherine
Oscar de la Renta dress
House of Lavande earrings
Vintage purse from The Way We Wore
W3 black sparkle pumps

PICNIC

Hillary
Topshop romper
Alice + Olivia cardigan
A.P.C. hat
Banana Republic purse
W3 denim espadrille wedges

Katherine
Ulla Johnson top
A.P.C. skirt
Benjamin sunglasses
Chan Luu bracelet
Forever 21 purse
W3 sneakers

POLO & HORSE RACES

Hillary
Vintage dress
Hobo belt
Vintage necklace from The Way We Wore
Vintage Yves Saint Laurent hat
Forever 21 earrings
Vintage Valentino clutch from The Way We Wore
W3 nude pumps

Katherine
Lucca Couture dress
Aryn K jacket
Buji Baja at Calypso belt
Benjamin sunglasses
Jennifer Ouellette hat
W3 brown cutout pumps

RAIN

Hillary
A.P.C coat
Levi's dress
Gap belt
Chan Luu scarf
Falke tights
L.L. Bean bag
W3 black wellies

Katherine
American Apparel coat
Joie blazer
Joie sweater
James Jeans
Ulla Johnson snood
L.L. Bean socks
W3 black buckle booties

RELIGIOUS OCCASION: DAY

Hillary
Vintage dress
Burberry trench
Club Monaco belt
Rachel Leigh earrings
Vintage Ferragamo purse
W3 nude pumps

Katherine
Silence & Noise cardigan
Ulla Johnson top
Oscar de la Renta skirt
Melinda Maria earrings
Chloe purse
W3 gray pumps

RELIGIOUS OCCASION: NIGHT

Hillary
Jeffrey Monteiro dress
Adrianna Papell jacket
Skova necklace
Falke tights
Arianne Tunney clutch
W3 black sparkle pumps

Katherine
RM by Roland Mouret jacket
Topshop top
The Row skirt
Kenneth Jay Lane necklace
JJ Winters clutch
W3 green snake print peep-toe pumps

REUNION: FAMILY

Hillary
Topshop dress
Rodarte for Target jacket
Yarnz scarf
Vintage Ferragamo purse
W3 black buckle booties

Katherine
Acne Dress
Marc Jacobs jacket
Elegantly Waisted belt
Forever 21 earrings
Vita ring
Perrin Paris clutch
W3 black lace-up booties

REUNION: SCHOOL

Hillary
Vintage Herve Leger dress from
The Way We Wore
Vintage cuffs
Armani clutch
W3 black platform peep-toe pumps

Katherine
Vintage jacket from The Way We Wore
Katy Rodriguez dress
CC Skye cuff
Succarra earrings
Rebecca Minkoff purse
W3 black sparkle pumps

ROAD TRIP

Hillary
Ecote at Urban Outfitters jacket
Current/Elliott top
291 tank
Vintage skirt
Bird bag
Benjamin sunglasses
Bird bag
W3 multi-color beaded t-strap sandals

Katherine
Topshop top
Nobody shorts
Karen Walker sunglasses
Giles & Brother bracelet
Forever 21 purse
W3 black and silver t-strap sandals

SHOPPING

Hillary
Club Monaco jacket
291 screen-print tee
Current/Elliott jeans
Luv AJ necklace
Jerome Dreyfuss bag
W3 gray ankle boots

Katherine
Raquel Allegra slip dresses
Ulla Johnson jacket
House of Harlow necklace
Benjamin sunglasses
Mulberry purse
W3 chain-detail sandals

SIGHTSEEING

Hillary
Barbour jacket
Saint James shirt
Citizens of Humanity jeans
A.P.C. scarf
Urban Outfitters sunglasses
Charles David purse
W3 sneakers

Katherine
A.P.C. top
Joe's Jeans shorts
A.P.C. hat
Chan Luu bracelets
Kimchi Blue bag
W3 black multi-color beaded t-strap sandals

SOMBER OCCASION

Hillary
Jovovich-Hawk dress
Bing Bang earrings
Marni bag
W3 black platform peep-toe pumps

Katherine
Shakuhachi dress
Chloe sunglasses
Rachel Leigh bangle
Spanx stockings
Givenchy clutch
W3 black cutout pumps

SPORTING EVENT

Hillary
Vintage Wickiling jacket
H&M top
Current/Elliott jeans
Shopbop hat
Chan Luu scarf
Gap belt
Jerome Dreyfuss bag
W3 gray wedges

Katherine
Simone jacket
Plastic Island sweater
Alternative Apparel tank
Iro skirt
Donna Karan tights
Mulberry bag
W3 gray lace-up boots

THEATER & PLAYHOUSE

Hillary
Vintage dress
Jenni Kayne belt
Chan Luu ring
JJ Winters clutch
W3 brown cutout pumps

Katherine
Shakuhachi dress
Raquel Allegra coat
Club Monaco belt
Jules Smith earrings
Chan Luu ring
Perrin Paris clutch
W3 gray lace-up boots

TRAVELING

Hillary
Burberry trench
T Los Angeles top
Serfontaine jeans
Chan Lulu scarf
KBL sunglasses
Rebecca Minkoff purse
W3 gray booties

Katherine
Zadig & Voltaire cardigan
Paul & Joe Sister shirt
Enza Costa sweater
Rag & Bone pants
Chan Luu scarf
Benjamin sunglasses
La Mer Collections watch
Mulberry purse
W3 gray flat ankle boots

WEDDING: BLACK-TIE

Hillary
Monqiue Lhuillier gown
House of Lavande ring
Vintage purse from The Way We Wore
W3 black platform peep-toe pumps

Katherine
Vintage dress from The Way We Wore
House of Lavande bracelet
W3 black sparkle pumps

WEDDING: COCKTAIL

Hillary
Versus dress
Falke tights
Vintage earrings from The Way We Wore
Vintage bracelet from The Way We Wore
Lauren Merkin clutch
W3 black platform peep-toe pumps

Katherine
Nuj Novakhett dress
CC Skye bangle
Lia Sophia bangle
Vintage earrings
Vintage bag from The Way We Wore
W3 black sparkle pumps

WEDDING: DAYTIME

Hillary
Milly Dress
Chan Luu scarf
Forever 21 sunglasses
Vintage bracelet
JJ Winters clutch
W3 nude pumps

Katherine
Jasmine Di Milo dress
Club Monaco belt
Bing Bang earrings
Bing Bang bracelets
Bird clutch
W3 gray wedges

WEEKEND

Hillary
Ecote at Urban Outfiters jacket
H&M shirt
Monrow skirt
Yarnz scarf
Benjamin sunglasses
Jerome Dreyfuss bag
W3 gray flat ankle boots

Katherine
Current/Elliott overalls
Equipment shirt
BCBG trench coat
La Mer Collections watch
Be & D purse
W3 black cutout lace-ups

ACKNOWLEDGMENTS

We were lucky enough to have some incredible support in the making of *What to Wear, Where*. First and foremost, we'd like to thank our amazing team at Who What Wear: Mika Onishi, Shayna Kossove, Liza Kaplan, Christian David, Jessica Baker, and Sarah Lee. You all go above and beyond for us every day and your efforts made this book possible—we appreciate it so much. That said, we'd like to give special thanks to Liza Kaplan, who was so instrumental in making sure the production of this book went smoothly. We'd also like to recognize the extended Who What Wear family for all their help in building this company: Jordan Bromley, Daniel Assael, Rob Dabney, Karla Robleto, and Richard Benn. Most of all, thank you to all the WhoWhatWear.com readers and subscribers for making this book possible!

Much love to Laurie Trott for her incredible taste, talent, and styling expertise. A huge thank you to Angela Fink, Nikki Tavdi, Faith Kensington, and Daniella Alberni for all their hard work, both on set and off. We are also eternally indebted to Erin Smith, Jen Atkin, Scott Cuhna, John D., and Barbara Warner for their beauty expertise and for always making us feel fabulous. And thanks to Rachel Mansfield and Bijou for their memorable contribution, too!

We are so grateful to have worked with our favorite photographer, Justin Coit, plus his amazing colleagues Nick Walker, Frank Terry, and Christine Hilberg. Justin, we are so lucky to have you as a part of the Who What Wear team—thank you for sharing your talent with us.

A special thanks to Nicole Richie, who has always been so supportive and wrote the most amazing foreword for this book. It's always an honor to work with you.

Huge thanks to our lovely editor Rebecca Kaplan, the entire team at Abrams, and the amazing Brett Ramey, our brilliant book designer. We're also so grateful for all the guidance and support we've received from our literary agents, Nena Madonia and Jan Miller. Additionally, we'd like to acknowledge and thank Adam Goldenberg and Don Ressler from JustFabulous for giving us the opportunity to create our shoe collection, W3 by Who What Wear.

This book couldn't have happened without the support of all of our favorite stores, including Shopbop, The Way We Wore, Neiman Marcus, My Theresa, Revolve, Net-A-Porter, and Pink Mascara. Many thanks to the numerous brands who were kind enough to participate and collaborate on this project—we are forever indebted to you!

On a personal note, we'd like to recognize Todd Ashley, Norma Gustafson, John and Carole Kerr, Riley Patricof and the Patricof family, Nelson Power-Coit, Sophia Rossi, and Kit and Doug West for all their support, love, and patience.

Finally, we'd like to conclude these acknowledgments with a special note for Nina Lenders, who was instrumental in the making of this book. In addition to your incredible taste and talent, you went above and beyond in so many ways. Thank you for always being available for brainstorming sessions, and for your endlessly creative and cute ideas and incredible efficiency, all of which made the looks in the this book the best they could be. We adore and appreciate you so much.

Editor: Rebecca Kaplan
Designer: Brett Ramey
Production Manager: Alison Gervais

Library of Congress Cataloging-in-Publication Data:
Kerr, Hillary.
 What to wear, where : the how-to handbook for any style situation /
Hillary Kerr and Katherine Power ; foreword by Nicole Richie
     p. cm.
 Includes bibliographical references and index.
 ISBN 978-0-8109-9703-5 (alk. paper)
 1. Women's clothing. 2. Fashion design. 3. Lifestyles. 4. Special
events. I. Power, Katherine. II. Title.
 TT507.K41998 2011
 746.9'2—dc22
                    2010037688

Printed in the USA
10 9 8 7 6 5 4 3 2 1

Abrams Image books are available at special discounts when
purchased in quantity for premiums and promotions as well as fund-
raising or educational use. Special editions can also be created to
specification. For details, contact specialmarkets@abramsbooks.
com or the address below.

THE ART OF BOOKS SINCE 1949
115 West 18th Street
New York, NY 10011
www.abramsbooks.com